TAWḤĪD ACCORDING TO SUFIS

The Oneness of God in Sufism

Compiling, Editing, Translating, and Commentary

Louay Fatoohi

SAFIS PUBLISHING

Birmingham – UK

Published in the United Kingdom by
Safis Publishing Limited, Birmingham, UK.
www.safispub.com

ISBNs
Paperback (Amazon KDP): 978-1-906342-57-9
Paperback (Lightning Source): 978-1-906342-58-6
Kindle: 978-1-906342-59-3
EPUB: 978-1-906342-60-9

First Edition
Version Identifier: 25040201

In the name of Allah,
the Gracious, the Merciful

Allah witnesses that there is no God except Him, and so do the angels and those of knowledge—that He is acting in justice. There is no God except Him, the invincible, the wise (Āl ʿImrān 3:18).

The best that I and the prophets before me have said is, "there is no God except Allah, (He is) alone, without a partner" (*Mālik, Al-Muwaṭṭaʾ, 726*).

Acknowledgements

Due to time constraints, I asked my brother, Faiz, for help with compiling Sufi quotes from some of the sources I used in the book. Without Faiz's generous help, the book would have taken much longer to complete.

As is the case with all of my writings, this book has greatly benefited from the comments and suggestions of my beloved wife, Dr Shetha Al-Dargazelli. Shetha has contributed significantly to improving the book.

Special thanks to my colleague Fatima Kasujee, whose excellent editing has greatly improved the book's clarity and readability.

I would like to express my gratitude and deep appreciation to Shetha, Faiz, and Fatima for helping me with this book. The Prophet (PBUH) said, "A person cannot be grateful to Allah if he is not grateful to people".[1]

---

[1] Al-Bukhārī, *Al-Adab al-mufrad,* 218.

Table of Contents

Book Idea

My interest in Sufism, both study and practice, spans over three and a half decades. In the middle of April 1988, I took the pledge of Ṭarīqa ʿAliyya Qādiriyya Kasnazāniyya (Ṭarīqa Kasnazāniyya) at the central takya in Baghdad, Iraq. [1] At the time, Shaikh Muḥammad al-Muḥammad al-Kasnazān (may Allah sanctify his secret) (1938-2020) was the Master of Ṭarīqa Kasnazāniyya.[2]

My first involvement in a Sufi literary work was in 1989. Shaikh Muḥammad al-Muḥammad had edited manuscripts of the book *Jilāʾ al-Khāṭir* by Shaikh ʿAbd al-Qādir al-Jīlānī, so I was asked to check and correct the proofs before the book went to press.

Since then, I have authored seven books about Sufism, most of which have been published in both Arabic and English. In addition to discussing Sufism in general, my books focus on the thought and practice of Ṭarīqa Kasnazāniyya and documenting the history of its Shaikhs, in particular, Muḥammad al-Muḥammad al-Kasnazān, whom I had the honour of closely accompanying.

I have also co-translated with my wife, Dr Shetha al-Dargazelli, *Jilāʾ al-Khāṭir* into English under the title *Purification of the Mind.* The book was first published in 1998, and it is currently in its third edition. In 2014, I edited and published manuscripts of an Arabic translation of a Persian book by Shaikh ʿAbd al-Qādir al-Jīlānī titled *Khamsata ʿAshrata Maktūban,* to which I added a commentary. The following year, I published an English translation of this book under the title *Fifteen Letters.*

In addition to my Sufi works, I have published, in both Arabic and English, books and research papers on Islamic studies. I have focused, in particular, on the historical miracles in the Qur'an and

---

[1] I have published a detailed introduction to the thought and history of Ṭarīqa Kasnazāniyya, *Al-Taṣawwuf fil-ṭarīqa al-ʿalīyya al-qādiriyya al-kasnazāniyya.*

[2] For a biography of Shaikh Muḥammad al-Muḥammad, see my book *A Life of love for the Prophet Muḥammad (PBUH).*

comparative Abrahamic religions. In each case, the idea of the publication was born out of my studies of the respective subject and new findings that I considered to be worthy contributions to the literature.

The source of the idea of this book, however, is completely different from all of my previous publications. Near dawn on Sunday 26 December 2021, I saw in a dream the Arabic phrase *al-Tawḥīd ʿinda al-ṣūfiyya* (the affirmation of Oneness according to Sufis). I understood it to be the title of a book that had not been written yet. I also realised that the book would consist of sayings by Sufi Shaikhs about tawḥīd. I felt that I had woken up just after seeing the dream. The first thing that occurred to me was that such a book would be merely a listing of similar sayings by different Sufis. I quickly realised that this would not be the case and that the title I saw could be made into an informative and enjoyable book. It was clear that the objective of the book would be to confirm the essentiality of tawḥīd for Sufis through their own words and refute the accusations against some Sufis that they held beliefs that contravened tawḥīd.

Implementing the idea went through the same process as my other works. I specified the objectives, identified the target readership, chose the subjects to cover, and designed a structure that presented the content in a logical way.

I hope that the book has aptly realised the dream.

The Content

I have decided that it is necessary to start the book with a chapter about Sufism and another about tawḥīd. The former discusses the etymology, history, and meaning of Sufism. The chapter on tawḥīd first explains the centrality of this concept in Islam and Sufism and then presents a critical analysis of the misguided and misleading accusations of the tawḥīd of some Sufis.

The rest of the book, which is its main content, consists of Sufi sayings about tawḥīd, which I have compiled from various sources and to which I have added an explanatory commentary. The individuals whom I have quoted in this book are described as Sufis in primary Sufi books. In the case of later Sufis, their practice of Sufism is known from their lives and writings.

The Sufi Quotes

I have focused on compiling Sufi sayings on tawḥīd from the earliest sources on Sufism, hence most of the quoted Sufis are from the third and fourth centuries of Hijra (ninth and tenth centuries CE). Some are well known and are quoted extensively in the sources, including on the subject of tawḥīd, whereas others are little known and are quoted only once on the subject of this book. I have added sayings of known Sufis from later centuries, concluding those Sufi luminaries with my Shaikh, Muḥammad al-Muḥammad al-Kasnazān.

I have dedicated a chapter to each Sufi and listed them in chronological order. I have used the first footnote in each chapter to specify when that Sufi lived, to locate him in time relative to the first generations of Muslims and to the eras of later Shaikhs and scholars. I have also added very brief biographical details, including naming some of those that the Sufi accompanied and learned from.

I have chosen this method because it realises the vision of the book in expounding the fundamental position of tawḥīd in Sufism throughout its history. Sufism represents the spiritual side of Islam, and as the oneness of Allah is the first of the two foundations of Islam, the second of which is the prophethood of Muḥammad (PBUH), it is essential in Sufism as well.

The oneness of God is a very simple concept denoting the fact that there is one Lord who created everything. But secondary, profound concepts derive from it, such as the names and attributes of the one Creator and the relationship of the creation with Him. The details of these derivative concepts cannot be captured in a few sayings, hence the idea of this book is to compile many different quotes. The Sufi sayings that I have selected explain various aspects of tawḥīd, providing a rich explanation of the first and last, most hidden and most manifest, greatest and most beautiful truth, "There is no God except Allah" (Muḥammad 47:19).

There are countless Sufi Shaikhs I could have quoted on tawḥīd. I could have also quoted more sayings of the Sufis I have chosen. I have limited the compilation to what I considered to be sufficient to convey the Sufi thought on tawḥīd to fulfil the objective of the book.

Naturally, there are similarities between the meanings of some sayings even though they express them differently. Yet the beauty of these words more than justifies quoting them all. Many of these Sufi sayings have poetic romance as they describe the Oneness of the worshipped Beloved and exalt Him. Sufi words are often a charming blend of knowledge and beauty, a unique fusion of intellectual endeavours, expressions of faith, feelings of the heart, and spiritual experiences.

The Sources

I have used two types of sources, those that contain the words of individual Sufis and others that collate sayings of many Sufis. The earliest sources of the first type are as follows:

- *Nahj al-balāgha*, ʿAlī Ibn Abī Ṭālib (d. 40/661)
- *Rasāʾl al-Junayd*, al-Junayd al-Baghdādī (d. 215/831)

- *Al-Mawāqif* and *al-Mukhāṭabāt*, Muḥammad Ibn ʿAbd al-Jabbār al-Niffarī (d. 354/965)

No early source of this kind was authored by the Sufi whose sayings it documents. Rather, it was compiled later, at times several centuries after him. I have quoted from each book some of the sayings on tawḥīd.

The earliest books that quote many Sufis and use the terms "Sufi" and "Sufism" are the following:

- *Al-Lumaʿ fī al-taṣawwuf*, Abū Naṣr al-Sarrāj al-Ṭūsī (d. 378/988)
- *Al-Taʿarruf li-madhhab ahl al-taṣawwuf*, Abū Bakr al-Kalābādhī (d. 380/990)
- *Ṭabaqāt al-ṣūfiyya*, Abū ʿAbd al-Raḥmān al-Sulamī (d. 412/1022)
- *Ḥilyat al-awliyāʾ wa ṭabaqāt al-aṣfiyāʾ*, Abū Nuʿaym al-Aṣfahānī (d. 430/1038)
- *Al-Risāla al-qushayriyya*, Abū al-Qāsim al-Qushayrī (d. 465/1073)
- *Kashf al-maḥjūb*, ʿAlī Abū al-Ḥasan al-Hujwīrī (d. 465/1073)

I have extracted from these sources most of the sayings about tawḥīd by various Sufis. When a saying is mentioned in more than one source, I used its wording in the earliest source, unless I deemed the version in the later source more accurate. I have listed the sayings of each Sufi in the chronological order of their respective sources.

At the end of the book, there is a bibliography of all the sources that I have used.

The Commentary

I have commented on every Sufi saying. The comments differ in length and detail. I have added each comment after the saying it explains. In some cases, often because of the length of the saying, I split the saying into parts and added a comment after each part. This division of the saying and commentary is clear from the context and from the fact that the end of every saying is followed by a mention of its source. I did not use footnotes for the comments but added them to the body text as this makes them easier to read, in particular, because some comments are rather long.

A comment elucidates ambiguities in the language, explains the meaning of the saying, or both. Earlier sayings are often in need of more explanation for one or more of three reasons. First, the saying appears without a context that helps in clarifying its meaning. This is particularly the case in works that compile sayings of multiple Sufis about a particular subject. The author is usually focused on collating sayings, without mentioning the context of the saying or explaining it. Second, the saying is terse, thus requiring explanation. Third, the text in the source is written without diacritical vowels, making it at times open to more than one reading.

The sayings of relatively later Sufis are usually clearer. For instance, the words of Shaikh ʿAbd al-Qādir al-Jīlānī (d. 561/1165) are taken from sermons he delivered at his school, which used to be attended by thousands of laypeople, in addition to scholars. On the other hand, some of the writings of Shaikh Ibn ʿAṭāʾ Allah al-Sakandarī (d. 709/1310) are clear but the quotes from *al-Ḥikam*, in particular, can contain ambiguity because of their brevity. I focused my commentary on explaining what may be ambiguous. I avoided repeating things mentioned in earlier comments.

A term may not have the exact same meaning in different Sufi writings. This also means that, at times, different Sufi terms overlap in meaning. This is not unexpected given that those Sufis are from different eras, some of which are separated by many centuries. The best and most comprehensive compilation of Sufi concepts and terms and their meanings is the unique encyclopedia, *Mawsūʿat al-kasnazān fīmā aṣṭalaḥ ʿalayh ahl al-taṣṣawuf wal-ʿirfān*, compiled by my Master, Shaikh Muḥammad al-Muḥammad al-Kasnazān.

Sufis and Sufism

As Sufis are the subject of this book, it is essential to provide an overview of the etymology, history, and meaning of "Sufi" and "Sufism".

Etymology

Scholars do not agree on the etymology of the term "Sufi". Abū Bakr al-Kalābādhī, the author of the second earliest book focused on Sufism, mentions four origins for this term. One is that it is derived from *ṣafā'* (purity or sincerity) of the innermost being of Sufis. For instance, Bishr Ibn al-Ḥārith al-Ḥāfī (d. 227/841) is reported to have said, "The Sufi is one whose heart *ṣafā* (has become pure) for Allah", and someone else is reported to have said, "The Sufi is one whose dealings with Allah *ṣafat* (have become sincere) so Allah (majestic and exalted is He) honoured him".

The term has also been related to the word *ṣaff* (rank or row), because "they are in the first *ṣaff* (row) before Allah (majestic and exalted is He) through the elevation of their determination to Him, turning their hearts towards Him, and standing with their innermost beings before Him". Others derived the term from *Ṣuffa*, which is an area at the back of the mosque of the Prophet (PBUH) that accommodated strangers and immigrants who did not have families or accommodations. Sufis are called so because their attributes are similar to those of the people of the *Ṣuffa*.

The fourth attribution is to *ṣūf* (wool) because of the asceticism of Sufis.[1] This opinion is favoured by Abū Naṣr al-Sarrāj al-Ṭūsī (d. 378/988), the author of the earliest book on *taṣawwuf* (Sufism) and Sufis, because "wearing wool clothing is a tradition of the Prophets (peace be upon them) and an emblem of the walīs and the chosen".[2] But even if some early Sufis used wool for clothes or as a symbol,

[1] Al-Kalābādhī, *Al-Ta'arruf*, 5.

[2] Al-Ṭūsī, *Al-Luma'*, 40-41.

that was the case with only a small minority. Abū al-Qāsim al-Qushayrī finds all these derivations to be weak because "there is no evidence to support an Arabic analogy or derivation of this term".[1]

Terminology

Some think that using the term *Ṣūfī* (Sufi) as a title for individuals perhaps goes back to the first half of the second century of Hijra. Historian Ibn al-Nadīm (d. 385/995) states that Jābir Ibn Ḥayyān, who is known as "the father of chemistry" and died at the end of the second century of Hijra, was known by the title "al-Ṣūfī" (the Sufi).[2] Some have doubted that Jābir Ibn Ḥayyān ever existed, considering him a legendary figure, but Ibn al-Nadīm rejected this claim.[3] According to ʿAbd al-Raḥmān al-Jāmī (d. 898/1424), the first individual to carry this title was Abū Hāshim al-Kūfī al-Ṣūfī, who died in 150/767, whose well-known ascetic contemporary, Sufyān al-Thawrī, acknowledged his influence on him.[4] However, al-Ṭūsī attributes to al-Ḥasan al-Baṣrī (d. 110/728) saying that he saw "a Sufi in the circumambulation" of the Kaʿba.[5] This indicates that the term "Sufi" was used as a description from as early as the end of the first century or the beginning of the second century of Hijra at the latest.

Mālik Ibn Anas (d. 179/795) is reported to have used the term in a verbal form, "Anyone who learns the law (*tafaqqah*) but does not practise Sufism (*taṣawwaf*) commits disobedience (*tafassaq*). Anyone who practises Sufism but does not learn the law leaves Islam (*tazandaq*). Anyone who combines both attains realisation (*taḥaqqaq*)". Many question the attribution of this saying to Mālik

---

[1] Al-Qushayrī, *Al-Risāla al-qushayriyya*, 464.

[2] Ibn al-Nadīm, *Al-Fihrast*, 498.

[3] One recent author who denied that Jābir Ibn Ḥayyān ever existed is Kāmil Muṣṭafā al-Shībī, *Al-Ṣila bayn al-taṣawwuf wa al-tashayyuʿ*, 268.

[4] Al-Jāmī, *Nafaḥāt al-uns* 66–67.

[5] Al-Ṭūsī, *Al-Lumaʿ*, 42.

because it is not found in his writings and is mentioned only in late sources.[1]

The term *mutaṣawwuf* has also become common. *Ṣūfī* refers to the seeker who has long been leading a Sufi life, whereas *mutaṣawwuf* is a novice in Sufism. A *mutaṣawwuf* is someone who works and aspires to become a *Ṣūfī*.

Meaning

Regardless of the many opinions about the etymology of "Sufism", its meaning in the primary sources is clear. It denotes having the noblest behaviours and states that draw the servant near to Allah. Various virtuous character attributes have come to be included under this term. For instance, al-Ṭūsī says, "having discharged the obligations and shunned prohibitions", Sufis are distinguished by the following:

> Abandoning what is of no concern to them and cutting off every relation that stands between them and their sought after and end goal. For they do not seek or have a goal other than Allah (blessed and Almighty is He).

He then says that they have "various etiquettes and states", including:

> Being content with little of this world instead of much; seeking only indispensable provision; being satisfied with little of this world's necessities of clothing, bedding, food, and others; choosing poverty over wealth; embracing scarcity and avoiding abundance; preferring hunger over satiety and little over much; abandoning haughtiness and aloofness; sacrificing prestige; having compassion for creatures; being humble with the insignificant and the dignitary; showing selflessness when needed; being disinterested in those obssessed with worldly gains; thinking well of Allah; sincerely hurrying to acts of obedience; rushing to doing all good things; turning towards Allah Almighty

---

[1] The earliest source that I have found that attributes this saying to Mālik is by Aḥmad Zarrūq al-Fārisī (d. 899 H/1493 CE), *Qawāʿid al-taṣawwuf*, 25.

and being in seclusion with Him; being steadfast in His trials and content with His decree; patiently maintaining self-discipline and opposing vagary; setting aside the fortunes of the self and opposing it, as Allah Almighty described it as evil-commanding,[1] and seeing it as the worst enemy between your two sides,[2] as the Messenger of Allah (PBUH) is reported to have said.[3]

Al-Ṭūsī goes on to detail the Sufis' etiquettes and good qualities.

Sufis have stressed that honouring all obligations of Sharīʿa is the foundation of the Sufi character and behaviour. This is why sayings such as the following words of Mālik Ibn Anas are often cited by them, "Anyone who learns the law but does not practise Sufism commits disobedience. Anyone who practises Sufism but does not learn the law leaves Islam. Anyone who combines both attains realisation". Sufis have approved of and preferred actions that take the servant farther from this world and its pleasures and nearer to Allah. They have demanded of themselves more than the minimum requirements of Sharīʿa. They usually refer to these two different states as *rukhṣa* (concession) and *ʿazīma* (strictest adherence), or "general concession" and "special concession", respectively. The following experience, narrated by Shaikh ʿAbd al-Qādir al-Jīlānī, explains the state of strict adherence, i.e., special concession, that Sufis demand of themselves:

One day I passed through a village surrounded by fields of corn. I stretched out my hand and picked a corn cane to suck. At that point, two men from the village, each holding a stick, came and beat me up until I collapsed to the ground. So I gave a pledge to Allah (majestic and exalted is He) at that moment not to take advantage again of the allowed concessions or avail myself of what is not mine. The law has

---

[1] "I do not exonerate myself; surely the self commands committing evil, except such as my Lord bestows mercy on; my Lord is forgiving, merciful" (Yūsūf 12:53).

[2] "Your worst enemy is your self that is between your two sides" (Al-Bayhaqī, *Al-Zuhd al-kabīr*, 343.)

[3] Al-Ṭūsī, *Al-Lumaʿ*, 29.

> allowed the person who passes by fields of plants and fruit to eat as much as he needs without paying anything in return and without taking away anything. This is a general concession. However, I was not allowed to take advantage of this concession and I was ordered to follow the strictest adherence (to the law) and meticulously apply pious restraint.[1]

Instead of complaining about being assaulted by the two men for exercising his legal right, Shaikh ʿAbd al-Qādir saw what happened as a reminder that he is one of those who should not avail themselves of the concessions of Sharīʿa for general Muslims. Rather, he must abide by the caution and pious restraint of the elect. For instance, he could not rule out that the corn was not planted on usurped land or farmed by labourers whose wages had not been paid, in which case it would have the toxicity of illegality.

Like learning other Islamic sciences, practising Sufism requires accompanying an experienced Master of it to learn from him. Companionship in Sufism is even more essential than in other sciences because Sufism is not just an intellectual and informational science; it is a behavioural and experiential science for purifying the soul from faults and adorning it with beautiful attributes. Studying Sufism without practising it does not make a person a Sufi because Sufism is knowledge and practice. Therefore, Sufis often cite the profound story of Moses and Khaḍir to explain the specific nature of companionship and learning in Sufism.[2]

---

[1] Al-Jīlānī, *Purification of the Mind*, 36-37.

[2] Fatoohi, *Shaikh Muhammad al-Muhammad al-Kasnazan*, 15-27.

Tawḥīd

Before studying sayings of Sufis about tawḥīd, this is a brief introduction to the status of tawḥīd in Islam and how Sufis have approached it. The chapter concludes with a discussion of how some Sufis have had their tawḥīd unfairly questioned.

The Foundation of Islam

The belief in the oneness of Allah is the cornerstone of Islam, as the most basic definition of Islam is the submission to the one Creator. Allah's words, "There is no God except Allah" (Muḥammad 47:19), describe this preexistent and eternal truth. Allah's articulation of the second testimony of Islam, "Muḥammad is the Messenger of Allah" (al-Fatḥ 48:29), points to the widest and last door to tawḥīd.

The Qur'an expresses various aspects of Allah's oneness in many verses. He is described as Wāḥid (One), "Indeed, Allah is only one god" (al-Nisā' 4:171); the Creator of everything that existed, exists, and will exist, "Allah is the Creator of everything" (al-Zumar 39:62); the Owner of and King over everything, "He in whose hand is the realm of all things" (Yāsīn 36:83); the Provider for the creation, "There is no moving creature on earth but its sustenance is on Allah" (Hūd 11:6); the One with the supreme will, "Indeed, Allah does what He wants" (al-Ḥajj 22:14); and other attributes of His oneness.

The Qur'an also draws attention to the fact that had there been more than one god, there would not have been this consistency and harmony in the creation, natural laws, and the universe in general, "And there has never been a god with Him. Otherwise, each god would have taken away what he created, and some of them would have been superior to others. Exalted is Allah above what they describe" (al-Mu'minūn 23:91). The continuity of the creation is itself a proof on the oneness of God, "Had there been in them (the heavens and earth) gods other than Allah, they both would have been ruined. So exalted is Allah, the Lord of the

Throne, above what they describe" (al-Anbiyā' 21:22).

The essentiality of tawḥīd in Islam is also manifested in the Qur'an's description of associating others with Allah (*shirk*), which is the opposite of tawḥīd, as being the only sin that Allah Almighty would not forgive, "Indeed, Allah does not forgive association with Him but He forgives what is less than that for whom He wills. He who associates others with Allah has gone far astray" (al-Nisā' 4:116). The phrase "what is less than that" confirms that assigning divinity to other than Allah is the gravest sin.

Naturally, there are many ḥadīths about tawḥīd. In a ḥadīth that confirms that it is the essence of the message of every prophet, the Messenger (PBUH) described the remembrance of "there is no God except Allah, alone, without a partner" as "the best that I and the prophets before me have said".[1] He also said about the testimony of tawḥīd, "Allah has prohibited for the Fire he who says 'there is no god except Allah', seeking Allah's pleasure".[2]

Tawḥīd was manifested in all of the actions, sayings, and states of the Prophet (PBUH), teaching the Muslims, who take him as their example, to follow him and embody tawḥīd in word and deed. For instance, he said about praying during ablution, "None of you would perform ablution so that it would reach all intended parts of the body and recite the following supplication, 'I testify that there is no god except Allah and that Muḥammad is His servant and Messenger' but would have the eight gates of paradise opened for him so he may enter through whichever he wishes".[3] His words of response to the call of pilgrimage were, "Here I am, O Allah, here I am! Here I am, O Allah, You have no partner, here I am! Surely, praise and blessing are Yours, as is kingship. You have no partner".[4] At times of grief, he used to say, "There is no god except

---

[1] Mālik Ibn Anas, *Al-Muwaṭṭa'*, 627.

[2] Al-Bukhārī, *Al-Ṣaḥīḥ,* 419.

[3] Muslim, *Al-Ṣaḥīḥ,* 234.

[4] Mālik Ibn Anas, *Al-Muwaṭṭa'*, 1192.

Allah, the Great, the Forbearing. There is no god except Allah, the Lord of the great Throne. There is no god except Allah, the Lord of the heavens, the Lord of the earth, and the Lord of the honourable Throne".[1]

The essentiality of the oneness of Allah in the Qur'an and the Sunna of the Prophet Muḥammad (PBUH) is absolutely clear, hence it has been a subject of consensus of all Muslim scholars throughout the centuries, regardless of their credal affiliations. None have denied that Allah's oneness is the foundation of Islam.

The term "tawḥīd" in Arabic has two close and connected meanings. It refers to the *belief* in the oneness of God and to *acting* in a way that reflects the belief that there is no god except Allah. Tawḥīd is the creature's confession, in belief and deed, of the oneness of the Creator.

Before we study the reasoning and elaboration of scholars in detailing the concept of tawḥīd and Sufi sayings about it, there is an extremely important fact that must be highlighted. Allah revealed Islam to all people without exception. Being the foundation of Islam, tawḥīd must be a simple and clear concept that can be understood even by the simplest of people. Indeed, tawḥīd means submitting that there is no God except Allah. Differences among scholars are confined to derivative concepts of this unambiguous and simple primary fact.

The Heart of Sufi Thought and Practice

Before talking about what Sufis have said about tawḥīd, it is necessary to remember that Sufism is a way of life involving noble behaviours and states that draw the servant closer to his Lord. It is not a credal system that consists of specific views about the elements of faith, as is the case with theological schools such as Mu'tazilism and Ash'arism. But the words of Sufis show that they have adopted credal concepts that have traditionally been described

[1] Al-Bukhārī, *Al-Ṣaḥīḥ*, 6121.

as of Ahl al-Sunna (the people of Sunna).

Sufis have spoken a lot about the essentiality of tawḥīd in Islam. When explaining it in detail, Sufis have taken the Qur'an as their source and the Prophet (PBUH) as their example, as Allah obligated every Muslim, "There has certainly been for you in the Messenger of Allah a good example for anyone whose hope is in Allah and the Last Day and remembers Allah often" (al-Aḥzāb 33:21). For instance, Abū al-Qāsim al-Qushayrī wrote the following summary at the beginning of his famous epistle on Sufis, which he authored in 437/1045:

> The Shaikhs of this group have built the foundations of their affair on sound principles of tawḥīd. Thus, they have protected their beliefs from innovations and have followed the belief of the predecessors and the followers of the Sunna in embracing tawḥīd that has neither *tamthīl* (likening) nor *ta'ṭīl* (denying). They have known the rights to *qidam* (ancientness) and they have embodied the attribute of what comes into existence from nonexistence.[1]

Tamthīl, which al-Qushayrī says that Sufis have rejected, is likening Allah to anything. One form of *tamthīl* is *tajsīm* (anthropomorphism), which is to claim that Allah has a body. *Ta'ṭīl* is to deny the ancientness of Allah's *asmā'* (names), such as *'alīm* (knowledgable) and *ḥayy* (everliving), and the ancientness of the *ṣifāt* (attributes) of those names, such as *'ilm* (knowledge) and *ḥayāt* (life). Over half a century before al-Qushayrī, Abū Bakr al-Kalābādhī wrote that all Sufis agree that Allah is "described with all the attributes that He described Himself with, named with all the names that He named Himself with, ancient with His names and attributes, unlike the creation in any way".[2]

The Mu'tazilīs denied that Allah's names and attributes are ancient because, they argued, considering them preexistent means to associate something with Allah. They considered Allah

---

[1] Al-Qushayrī, *Al-Risāla al-qushayriyya*, 24.

[2] Al-Kalābādhī, *Al-Ta'arruf*, 13.

knowledgeable by Himself, not by knowledge; hearing by Himself, not by an ability to hear; and so on, although they differed in the details of their arguments.[1] Some sayings in this book mention, in the course of describing tawḥīd, the Sufis' rejection of the denial of the ancientness of Allah's names and attributes. ʿAlī Ibn al-Kātib (d. c. 340/951) has accurately summarised the disagreement between the Sufis and the Muʿtazilīs, saying, "The Muʿtazilīs have exalted Allah Almighty with the intellect, so they have erred, whereas the Sufis have exalted Him with knowledge, so they have been right".[2] Muʿtazilīs relied on the intellect to analyse Allah's names and attributes in the Qur'an, concluding that they could not be ancient.

Sufis, on the other hand, consider the intellect too limited to delve into the Divine Being and that exalting Allah as He deserves requires stopping the intellect at its limits and accepting Allah's description of Himself without excessive analysis. This recognition of the limitedness of human senses and cognition has made Sufis extremely cautious when talking about Allah. They often mention the creature's ignorance of the nature of the Creator; stress that He does not have a like, peer, companion, or opposite; and exalt Him absolutely over anything and everything. Tawḥīd for them combines the unknowability and indescribability of the essence of Allah, which is known as "apophatic or negative theology", with affirming His attributes and effects in His creation and their describability, that is, "cataphatic or positive theology". Therefore, Sufis often quote the following verse that beautifully combines denying *tamthīl* (likening) with confirming the attributes and names, "There is nothing like Him, and He is the hearing, the seeing" (al-Shūrā 42:11). Its first half, "There is nothing like Him",

---

[1] Al-Qāḍī ʿAbd al-Jabbār (d. 415/1025) explains the Muʿtazilī views in his book *Sharḥ al-uṣūl*, 149-297. See also ʿAbd al-Qāhir al-Baghdādī's (d. 429/1037) *Al-Farq bayn al-firaq*, 104, 288.

[2] Al-Qushayrī, *Al-Risāla al-qushayriyya*, 112.

denies likening Allah to anything, while its second half, "and He is the hearing, the seeing", confirms His names and attributes. Combining confirmatory and negatory language about Allah's attributes is also clear in this short chapter:[1]

> Say, "He, Allah, is One; Allah who is self-sufficient;[2] He has not begotten and He has not been begotten; and there has never been one equal to Him" (al-Ikhlāṣ 112:1-4).

Al-Qushayrī's words, "They have known the rights to ancientness", refer to the submission of the Sufis to the Lordship and Oneness of the preexistent and eternal Creator, Allah. *Qidam* (ancientness) is an attribute of Allah alone as everything else is *muḥdath* (originated), i.e., was created at some point. His statement, "They have embodied the attribute of what comes into existence from nonexistence", means that they have *willingly* adorned themselves with the attributes of servanthood, while everything is *forcibly* in a state of servanthood. After quoting Sufi sayings about tawḥīd, al-Qushayrī concluded his chapter about tawḥīd by saying, "The creeds of the Sufi Shaikhs agree with the statements of the people of the truth on foundational matters".[3]

Before continuing to discuss Sufi concepts, I would like to briefly clarify a critical point. The differences between Muslim scholars and groups about the names and attributes of Allah and other credal matters stem from differences in interpreting Qur'anic

---

[1] Some of the earliest scholars to write in detail about the many differences between Muslim theological schools, including the Muʿtazilīs, about subjects such as *tamthīl* and *taʿṭīl*, are Abū al-Ḥasan al-Ashʿarī (d. 330/941) in *Maqālāt al-Islāmiyyīn*. and ʿAbd al-Qāhir al-Baghdādī in *Al-Farq bayn al-firaq*.

[2] Scholars have suggested various meanings for Allah's name *al-ṣamad*, including "the One sought for all needs", "the One remaining after the vanishing of His creation", and "the One having no need of anyone while everyone needs Him". However, the meaning that I am inclined towards is "One who is self-sufficient", so He does not need others (Al-Qurṭubī, *Al-Asnā fī sharḥ asmāʾ Allah al-ḥusnā*, vol. 1, 177-186.)

[3] Al-Qushayrī, *Al-Risāla al-qushayriyya*, 36.

texts. These differences are natural because even when most people consider a text to be completely clear and capable of accommodating only one interpretation, there are always some who understand it differently, even if their alternative interpretations look absurd, improbable, or completely wrong to the majority. At times, different interpretations can be reconciled, indicating that the text has more than one meaning, but at other times, they are contradictory. That almost every text is given more than one interpretation is an undeniable reality attested in the writings of scholars. The disagreement is over which interpretation looks correct or more likely to be correct. Interpreting a Qur'anic text is an act of *ijtihād*, i.e., human reasoning, to understand a divine text. *Ijtihād* often leads to different interpretations. Accordingly, I believe in a principle that I abbreviate as *lā takfīr fī al-tafsīr* (there should be no accusation of disbelief because of interpretation).

This principle can also be derived from the fact that faith (*'īmān*) in the message of Muḥammad (PBUH) is built on six pillars, which are believing in each of Allah, His angels, His Books, His Messengers, the Last Day, and predestination (*qadar*). The following verse mentions five pillars in the context of judging those who deny them, "And whoever disbelieves in Allah, His angels, His Books, His Messengers, and the Last Day has certainly gone far astray" (al-Nisā' 4:136). The concept of predestination is mentioned in other verses, such as, "No calamity happens on the earth or to yourselves except that it is in a register before We bring it into being. That is easy for Allah" (al-Ḥadīd 57:22). The Prophet (PBUH) has also defined faith as follows, "to believe in Allah, His angels, His Books, His Messengers, and the Last Day, and to believe in predestination, good and bad".[1] An interpretation could not nullify the faith of the interpreter if it does not contravene any of the six pillars.

For Sufis, tawḥīd is in degrees, just like faith. The start of tawḥīd

---

[1] Muslim, *Al-Ṣaḥīḥ*, 8.

is confessing that there is no God other than Allah, and its ultimate degree is for the muwaḥḥid to see all creation, including himself, as an instrument in Allah's hand. 'Abd al-Qādir al-Jīlānī expressed this as follows:

> In the beginning, when faith is still weak, [the person says,] "There is no God except Allah". In the end, when faith has become strong, [the person says,] "There is no God except You" (al-Anbiyā' 21:87) because he addresses One who is present and seen".[1]

Sufi practice is the travel from the starting point of the tawḥīd by the tongue to the destination of the tawḥīd by witness. The seeker tries to go as far as he can on this spiritual journey.

Criticism of and Accusations Against Sufis

Why, then, have some Sufis been criticised, had their tawḥīd questioned, and even been accused of disbelief? There are three main reasons. **First**, misunderstanding Sufis' descriptions of the state of *fanā'* or "spiritual annihilation". The latter denotes the complete submission to Allah, i.e., the perfect practice of Islam, which is the realisation of total servanthood, "I have not created the jinn and mankind except to worship Me" (al-Dhāriyāt 51:56). Abū Ḥāmid al-Ghazālī (d. 505/1111) has explained this misunderstanding, citing some of the best-known statements about spiritual annihilation whose meanings have been distorted:

> These intimate knowers agreed, having ascended to the heaven of reality, that they did not see in existence other than the Real Wāḥid. Some of them arrived at this state through knowledge while others experientially. The plurality of things became inexistent for them and they drowned in the absolute Oneness. Their intellects were taken by it so they became as if dumbfounded by Him. No capacity remained in them for remembering other than Allah, not even remembering themselves. Nothing other than Allah remained with them. They became intoxicated, such an intoxication that the control of their

---

[1] Al-Jīlānī, *Al-Fatḥ al-rabbānī*, assembly 62, 266.

> intellects was lost. So one of them said, "I am the Real One", another said, "Glory be to Me! How great my station is!", and another, "There is nothing in this robe other than Allah".[1]

Al-Ghazālī went on to add that the misunderstanding has resulted from treating metaphorical Sufi statements as if they were literal. Some Sufi speech is almost poetic prose, and the language of poetry is often metaphorical:

> The words of the lovers when they are in a state of intoxication should be concealed, not spoken out. When their intoxication has subsided and they have returned under the control of the intellect, which is Allah's scale on His earth, they realise that this was not true unification, but something similar to unification. It is like a lover saying under the influence of extreme love, "I am he whom I love and he whom I love is I".[2]

Such Sufi sayings are called *shaṭaḥāt*. Linguistically, *shaṭh* means to go far and continue to do so. When applied to Sufism, it means to move away from what is familiar. Al-Ṭūsī has defined the Sufi *shaṭḥa*, which is the singular of *shaṭaḥāt*, as, "An unfamiliar statement describing ecstasy that overflows with its power and erupts with its intense commotion and overpower".[3] It is a pronouncement that is alien to the ear and is articulated more by feelings than the intellect, at times because it is the fruit of a spiritual experience that is difficult to describe in a familiar way. A *shaṭḥa* is not the product of a false creed as claimed by some who misunderstand it or choose to approach it with suspicion and distrust. This is how al-Ḥallāj, for instance, complained of those who wronged him by misunderstanding his words and distorting

---

[1] The sayings, "I am the Real One" and "There is nothing in this robe other than Allah", are attributed to al-Ḥallāj (d. 309/922 CE), but al-Ghazālī suggests that they were by two different people. The saying, "Glory be to Me! How great my station is!", is attributed to Abū Yazīd al-Basṭāmī (d. 261/875).

[2] Al-Ghazālī, *Mishkāt al-anwār,* 139.

[3] Al-Ṭūsī, *Al-Luma',* 453.

them with interpretations that defy reason:

> What is it about me and people that they irrationally blame me?
> My religion is mine and people's religion is theirs.[1]

It is worth noting that some Sufis also have objected to some of what al-Ḥallāj said. Al-Sulamī has noted, "The Shaikhs differ about him. Most Shaikhs have rejected and denied him and have refused to accept that He has a standing in Sufism".[2] He did not name any of al-Ḥallāj's critics but he mentioned some of those who defended him. Al-Sulamī's inclusion of al-Ḥallāj in his book, a compilation of biographies and sayings of the greatest Sufis, means that he stood with those who rejected the accusations against al-Ḥallāj. ʿAbd al-Qādir al-Jīlānī, who is highly regarded by Sufis and non-Sufis alike, accurately analysed and summarised al-Ḥallāj's situation as follows, "Al-Ḥallāj tripped and there was no one in his time to give him a hand. Had I been in his time, I would have given him a hand". Describing al-Ḥallāj's *shaṭaḥāt* as merely a "trip" confirms the soundness of al-Ḥallāj's creed. At the same time, it indicates that some of his statements were open to serious misunderstandings that could have grave consequences. Shaikh ʿAbd al-Qādir confirmed this analysis in another comment about al-Ḥallāj.[3] It looks like Ibn Taymiyya referred to this opinion of al-Jīlānī when he summarised the view of those who defend al-Ḥallāj that, "He was a righteous man of proper behaviour but ecstasy and spiritual states overcame him so he tripped in his sayings and did not realise what he said".[4] Despite his severe criticism of some of al-Ḥallāj's sayings, Ibn Taymiyya stated that many have been falsely attributed to him and some have had more read into them than they really meant.[5]

Second, some Sufi writings contain considerable metaphorical

---

[1] Al-Ḥallāj, *Dīwān*, 180.

[2] Al-Sulamī, *Ṭabaqāt al-ṣūfiyya*, 236.

[3] Ibn al-Wardī, *Tārīkh*, 355-356.

[4] Ibn Taymiyya, *Al-Istiqāma*, vol. 1, 116.

[5] Ibn Taymiyya, *Al-Istiqāma*, vol. 1, 119.

and special language. One of the most famous examples is the writings of Muḥyī al-Dīn Ibn ʿArabī. When his writings are read by someone unfamiliar with his special concepts and expressions, misunderstanding his ambiguous writings becomes almost inevitable.

My Shaikh, Muḥammad al-Muḥammad al-Kasnazān, states in the introduction to his encyclopedia about Sufism that by the middle of the ninth century of Hijra (fifteenth century CE), Sufi writings had enriched Islamic literature with "a huge wealth of and countless terms and concepts", so much so that it is appropriate to say that "a complete religious language had developed, which is the 'Islamic Sufi language'". He goes on to note and criticise the "campaigns to distort the terms of this language and interpret them in a way that distances them from their true Islamic meanings".[1]

Third, taking the words of a Sufi out of the context of his other sayings, writings, and life as a whole. For instance, Ibn ʿArabī wrote extensively about the oneness and Lordship of Allah and the servanthood of everything and everyone to Him. Also, those Sufis lived a strict Islamic life and worshipped Allah much, which means, among other things, that they repeatedly proclaimed the testimony of tawḥīd, "There is no God except Allah". Questioning the soundness of the belief in the oneness of Allah of these people or attributing to them blasphemy, let alone accusing them of claiming divinity, is an absurdity that contravenes their words, behaviours, and states. Interpreting the words of any Sufi must be in the context of his overall thought and life. This is a basic right for every scholar and thinker.

This does not mean there have not been people who deceitfully claimed to be Sufis without emulating them in word and action. Indeed, as early as the first third of the fifth century of Hijra (eleventh century CE), al-Qushayrī complained that he wrote his book on Sufism because its people had become too few and many

[1] Al-Kasnazān, *Mawsūʿat al-kasnazān*, 53.

had falsely claimed to be Sufis yet they contradicted the Sufi way and attributed to Sufism things that are alien to it.[1]

Yet none of the well-known Sufis deserve such criticism. Also, it is important to differentiate between a strayed minority of claimants of Sufism and true Sufis, whose history goes back to the first generation of Muslims. Even Ibn Taymiyya, whose thought at times lacks flexibility and whose critical language can be too harsh, distinguished between false claimants of Sufism and true Sufis, whom he praised.[2] Indeed, his immense respect for Shaikh ʿAbd al-Qādir al-Jīlānī is seen in his recounting of karāmas (supernatural feats) of al-Jīlānī in his lifetime and after his death[3] and in his writing a commentary on al-Jīlānī's book *Futūḥ al-ghayb*. The fact that individuals may not truly represent the thought that they claim is a human condition that is found in all groups and denominations, religious and non-religious. Indeed, many self-appointed speakers for Islam have made false claims about it, so it is not fair or reasonable to take that as a shortcoming in Islam or fault Muslims in general for it.

After this introduction, we will start our journey through the words of Sufi Shaikhs with their first Master after the Prophet Muḥammad (PBUH), Imam ʿAlī Ibn Abū Ṭālib.

---

[1] Al-Qushayrī, *Al-Risāla al-qushayriyya*, 19-21.

[2] Ibn Taymiyya, *Majmūʿ fatāwa,* Book of "Taṣawwuf", vol. 11.

[3] Ibn Taymiyya, *Majmūʿ fatāwa,* Book of "Tawḥīd al-ulūhiyya", vol. 1, 172; Book of "ʿIlm al-sulūk", vol. 110, 549-550.

ʿAlī Ibn Abī Ṭālib[1]

Praise be to Allah whose due praise is out of the reach of speakers, whose favours cannot be counted by calculators, and whose true worth cannot be acknowledged by those who try their best to do so. He cannot be attained by any level of determination and cannot be comprehended by deep thinking.

No creature can estimate Allah with the estimation that is due to Him or know His reality with any amount of effort and thinking.

His attributes have no limits, known descriptions, set time, or appointed end. He brought the creatures into existence by His omnipotence, spread winds by His mercy, and made firm the expanse of the earth with rocks.

Allah's descriptions are absolute, not limited. They are ancient and eternal like His ancientness and eternality. They are the

[1] 23 BH-40 H / 599-661 CE. He grew up in the custody of the Prophet (PBUH) and was brought up by him. Sources agree that Khadīja bint Khuwaylid, the wife of the Prophet (PBUH), was the first woman to embrace Islam, but they differ on whether ʿAlī or Abū Bakr al-Ṣiddīq was the first Muslim man. It is only logical, however, that the Prophet (PBUH) would have informed his family first about his prophetic mission, which means that ʿAlī and Khadīja were the first Muslims. He is the only Companion of the Prophet (PBUH) to be referred to with the title *karrama Allahu wajhahu* (may Allah honour his face) because he never worshipped an idol. ʿAlī has a unique status with Sufis. With the exception of the Naqshabandī Ṭarīqa, which is traced to Abū Bakr, all Sufi Ṭarīqas go back to ʿAlī. He was the heir of the spiritual knowledge of the Prophet (PBUH) who said about him, among other things, "I am the city of knowledge and ʿAlī is its door, so whoever seeks the city, let him come to the door" (Al-Ḥākim al-Nisābūrī, *Al-Mustadrak*, 4637.)

attributes and names with which He described Himself in the Qur'an. He is unique in His attributes and names.

> The foremost in religion is knowing Him, the perfection of knowing Him is testifying Him, the perfection of testifying Him is tawḥīd, the perfection of tawḥīd is being sincere to Him, and the perfection of sincerity to Him is not describing Him because every description testifies that it is distinct from what it describes and everything that is described testifies that it is distinct from its description. So whoever describes Allah (glory be to Him) associates Him with something, and whoever assigns to Him an associate makes Him two. Whoever makes Him two splits Him. Whoever splits Him is ignorant of Him.

The Creator must not be described with transient attributes of the creation.

> Whoever is ignorant of Him alludes to Him. Whoever alludes to Him limits Him.

Only what is limited spatially and/or temporally is possible to point to.

> Whoever limits Him counts Him. Whoever says "wherein?" implies that He is contained. Whoever says "on what?" implies that there are things in which He is not present.

Allah is not inside or on something, but this does not mean there is no place where He is not present.

> He is extant but not by origination.

The Arabic term *ḥadath* means origination, happening,

occurrence, or creation at a point in time. Before that, the thing or matter did not exist. The opposite of *ḥadath* is *qidam*, which means "ancientness". The passive participle of the former is *muḥdath*, which means created or made at a certain point. The adjective of *qidam* is *qadīm*, which means "ancient". In such contexts, the latter refers to the ever-present whose existence has no beginning, i.e., Allah. We will encounter these two terms and concepts in a number of Sufi sayings.

> He exists but not out of nonexistence.

Denying Allah's existence by origination does not mean that He came into existence out of nothing. Rejecting all alternative possibilities of an issue when speaking about Allah, such as denying His existence of "thingness" or "nothingness", is a linguistic device that Sufis have often used to stress that we cannot think of Allah's existence using concepts that are familiar to us.

> He is with everything but without association, and He is away from everything but without separation.

He is present with everything without having a link to it, and He is far from everything without being separate from it.

> He acts but not with movements and instruments.

Unlike created things, His actions do not involve moving or using instruments.

> He sees yet none of His creation can look at Him. He is alone such that there is nothing in whose presence He would feel intimacy or in whose absence He would feel loneliness (*Nahj al-balāgha*, 1).[1]

---

[1] All quotes are from *Nahj al-balāgha* in which al-Sharīf al-Raḍī compiled speeches of Imam ʿAlī three and a half centuries after him. The number in the

His aloneness is such that He wouldn't find companionship or intimacy with something or miss its absence.

> Praise be to Allah who never had a condition that preceded another so He would be First before being Last or He would be Manifest before being Hidden.

Every originated thing is subject to change. This is Allah's law in His creation. The Ancient One, Allah, never changes. Any apparent contradiction between His attributes, such as being the First and the Last and the Hidden and the Manifest, is not a real one. Each one of Allah's beautiful names has unique meanings. These attributes are permanent, so they do not indicate that He has changing conditions.

> Everyone described as alone other than Him is little.

The aloneness of any creature indicates its weakness for having no helpers. This does not apply to Allah's aloneness because His absolute power has no source other than Him.

> Every invincible one other than Him is subjugated. Every powerful one other than Him is weak. Every master other than Him is enslaved. Every knowledgeable one other than Him is a knowledge-seeker. Every capable one other than Him is sometimes capable and sometimes incapable.

Only Allah's attributes are absolute, perfect, and permanent. Regardless of how great a creature's attributes are, they remain limited, imperfect, and subject to change because he is a servant under the rule of His Creator and Lord, "Everything will perish

---

source of each quote is the number of the speech, not its page number in the source.

except His face" (al-Qaṣṣaṣ 28:88).

> Every hearer other than Him is deaf to subtle sounds and is deafened by loud sounds, and distant sounds are inaccessible to him. Every sighted one other than Him is blind to hidden colours and subtle bodies.

Only Allah perceives everything, so He hears and sees everything.

> Every manifest thing other than Him is hidden and every hidden thing other than Him is not manifest.

Every manifest thing is a creature that points to its Creator, so it is hidden relative to Allah's absolute manifestation. Allah is the only hidden one who is also manifest because His creation comprises signs that point to Him.

> He did not create what He created to strengthen His authority, out of fear of the consequences of time, or to seek help against a warring peer, an arrogant partner, or a competing opponent. They are enslaved creatures and humbled servants.

He did not bring the creation into existence because He needed them to help Him against someone or something. Rather, He created them as humble servants who are in permanent need of their Lord, "I have not created the jinn and mankind except to worship Me. I do not want from them any provision, nor do I want them to feed Me" (al-Dhāriyāt 51:56-57).

> He has not dwelt in things to be said, "He is present in them", nor has He gone away from them to be said, "He is far from them".

He is near to things without mixing with them, and He is distant from them without separation from them.

> He is not fatigued by the creation of what He initiated or the management of what He made to multiply. He has no incapacity regarding what He created. No uncertainty has ever occurred to Him in what He decreed and apportioned. Rather, His decree is exquisite, His knowledge is perfect, and His commandment is unstoppable.

Creating and managing the creation does not tire Him. Nothing can stop what He wishes to do with His creation. He has total knowledge so nothing is uncertain to Him. His decree is flawless, His knowledge is absolute without any ignorance, and His order is done and no one can revoke it.

> He is the one wished for at the time of affliction and the one who is feared at the time of favour (*Nahj al-balāgha*, 63).

It is He whose mercy is hoped for during afflictions and whose punishment is feared when enjoying His blessings.

> No affair keeps Him busy, time does not change Him, space does not contain Him, and no tongue can describe Him (*Nahj al-balāgha*, 176).

Nothing occupies Him away from other things, He is not subject to time or space, and He is exalted over any description.

> Whoever ascribes to Him a condition does not affirm His oneness, whoever likens Him misses His reality, whoever claims He has any semblance does not truly refer to Him, and whoever alludes to and imagines Him does not truly mean Him.

Attributing a condition to Him contravenes tawḥīd, likening Him to something is going astray, and He cannot be the subject of resemblance, pointing to, or imagination.

> Everything that is known by itself is created. Everything that exists because of something else its existence has an external cause.

Every knowable thing is created and the existence of every existing thing depends on something else. Allah, on the other hand, cannot be known as things may be known, and He is self-supporting, so His existence does not depend on others.

> He acts without moving instruments, determines without using thoughts, and is rich without acquisition.

Unlike living beings and inanimate things, His action does not involve moving instruments, He plans without a process of thinking, and He is rich not because He acquires things. His attributes cannot be understood like those of His creation are.

> Times do not accompany Him nor do implements support Him. His being preceded times, His existence nonexistence, and His preexistence every beginning.

He is outside time, so He was before time, nonexistence, and all beginnings. He does not need help.

> By His making the senses perform their functions, it is known that He has no senses. By His making opposite matters, it is known that He has no opposite. By His making things associated with each other, it is known that He has no associate (*Nahj al-balāgha*, 184).

Being the creator of senses, opposites, and associates means that he has no senses, opposites, or associates.

Jaʿfar Al-Ṣādiq[1]

> Whoever claims that Allah is in something, came from something, or is on something commits polytheism. If He were on something, He would have been carried. If He were in something, He would have been confined. If He were from something, He would have been originated (*Al-Risāla al-qushayriyya*, 35).

Any spatial description of Allah is a form of polytheism because space is an attribute of creatures. Everything is originated whereas the Creator is preexistent and eternal.

---

[1] 80-148 H / 700-766 CE. He was the grandson of ʾAlī Zayn al-ʿĀbidīn, son of the martyred Imām Ḥusayn. His mother was a descendant of Abū Bakr al-Ṣiddīq. He is the sixth Imām of the Twelvers and the Ismāʿīlī Shia. Abū Ḥanīfa al-Nuʿmān and Mālik Ibn Anas were among his students. He has a juristic school named after him, the Jaʿfarī.

Aḥmad Ibn ʿĀṣim Al-Anṭākī[1]

Act as if there is no one on this earth other than you and no one in heaven other than Him (*Ṭabaqāt al-ṣūfiyya*, 120).

Do not occupy yourself with any creature on earth or from the spirit world, including angels, spirits, and jinn. Engross yourself only with being a servant of your Lord.

[1] 140-239 H / 758-854 CE. He lived in Damascus. He was a companion of Bishr al-Ḥāfī and Sarī al-Saqaṭī. He was called "the spy of hearts" for his power of insight.

Al-Ḥārith Ibn Asad Al-Muḥāsibī[1]

> Reckoning and weighing up are in four areas: between belief and disbelief, between sincerity and telling lies, between tawḥīd and polytheism, and between sincerity and hypocrisy (*Ṭabaqāt al-ṣūfiyya*, 60).

The spiritual state of a human being depends on what he acquires from four pairs of opposite attributes. A Muslim should endeavour to earn the good ones and avoid their opposites. The perfect Muslim combines belief, truthfulness, tawḥīd, and sincerity.

[1] 170-243 H / 787-858 CE. He was originally from Basra but died in Baghdad. His title is derived from "Muḥāsib", which means one who reckons, because he would hold himself to account so much. Al-Junayd al-Baghdādī is one of those who quoted him. Some of his many books have survived.

Dhū Al-Nūn al-Miṣrī[1]

[Tawḥīd] is to realise that: Allah's (exalted is He) power over things is without mixing (with them) and His fashioning of things is without an intermediary.

He manages His creation without mixing with it and without means.

His action is the cause of everything that occurs and comes into being but there is no cause for His action.

Natural laws, which govern the dead and the living, and the intelligence and capabilities of living creatures are the causes of everything that occurs in the universe. They are created by Allah, "And Allah has created you and what you make" (al-Ṣāffāt 37:96), and they do not happen without His permission, "And you do not will unless Allah, Lord of the worlds, wills" (al-Takwīr 81:29). On the other hand, Allah's creation of these causes has no cause other than His will, "Indeed, Allah does what He wills" (al-Ḥajj 22:18), and the divine will is unstoppable, "Indeed, your Lord is a doer of what He wants" (Hūd 11:107).

Neither in the upper heavens nor in the lower earths is there a disposer other than Allah (exalted is He). Whatever you may conceive with your imagination, Allah (exalted is He) is different from it (*Al-Luma*ʿ, 49).

Allah is incomprehensive to the intellect even by imagining.

A man asked him for advice, so he said, "If, in the knowledge of the unseen, you had been aided with truthful

---

[1] 179-245 H / 796-860 CE. His full name is Thūbān Ibn Ibrāhīm. He was born in Akhmīm and died in Giza, Egypt.

tawḥīd, then that is best for you. Before you were born, from Adam (peace be upon him) to this day, the call of the prophets and messengers preceded you. If you were not so, then how would a cry for help save those who are drowning?" (*Al-Luma'*, 335).

All prophets and messengers called people to tawḥīd. If a person is not a muwaḥḥid in Allah's knowledge, then no advice could benefit him. The person who is not a muwaḥḥid has no salvation.

I have not seen anything that urges the person to seek sincerity more than seclusion. When a person enters into seclusion, he does not see anyone other than Allah (exalted is He). When he does not see other than Him, nothing other than Allah's command would move him. The person who loves seclusion becomes attached to the column of sincerity and grasps a major pillar of truthfulness (*Ṭabaqāt al-ṣūfiyya*, 30).

The nearest route to sincerity in tawḥīd is seclusion (*khalwa*). In the absence of creatures, it is easier for the person to experience the reality that Allah is the only truly existent and that all creatures exist by His power. When a person in seclusion attains this state, he becomes a perfect Muslim, doing only what satisfies Allah. Retreat is the cornerstone of sincerity and an indispensable foundation of truthfulness. The Prophet Muḥammad (PBUH) used to go into seclusion before the revelation of the Qur'an. After the revelation, he used to perform night worship (*qiyām al-layl*), which is a retreat with Allah.

Be careful that you do not become cut off from Him so you become deceived… A deceived person is one who looks at His gifts, thus he stops looking at Him by looking at His gifts… People are attached to the means, whereas

> the truthful are attached to the owner of the means... The sign of their hearts' attachment to gifts is asking for gifts from Him, whereas one sign of the attachment of the heart of the truthful person to the Owner of gifts is the coming of gifts to him and his occupation with Him away from them... Be dependent on Allah in whatever state you are in, not on your state when dealing with Allah... Understand this, for it derives from the purity of tawḥīd (*Ḥilyat al-awliyāʾ*, vol. 9, 351).

Pure tawḥīd is to not be occupied away from Him by anything, including His favours, and to always have trust in Him, not only in certain states.

> When asked about Allah's (exalted is He) words, "the Gracious is settled on the Throne" (Ṭāhā 20:5), he replied, "He affirmed His being and denied having a location,

The verse confirms Allah's kingship and ownership of everything. It also refutes the thought that He exists in a specific location.

> for He exists by His very being. All things exist according to His command, as He (glorified is He) willed" (*Al-Risāla al-qushayriyya*, 34).

Allah is described as *wājib al-wujūd* (of necessary existence) because He is preexistent and eternal, so His existence has no beginning or end, "He is the First and the Last" (al-Ḥadīd 57:3), and His existence does not depend on someone or something else. Every creature, on the other hand, is *jāʾiz al-wujūd* (of possible existence), so they may or may not exist, depending on Allah's will.

Abū Yazīd al-Basṭāmī[1]

> Anyone who alludes to Him with *ʿilm* (knowledge) has fallen into disbelief because alluding with knowledge applies only to what is known. Anyone who alludes to Him with *maʿrifa* (intimate knowledge) has deviated because alluding with intimate knowledge applies only to what is limited (*Al-Lumaʿ*, 295).

Claiming to have *ʿilm* (knowledge) of Allah other than what He said about Himself in His revelation is disbelief because it is a false claim about Allah. Claiming to have *maʿrifa* (intimate knowledge) of Him is also a deviation from the truth because *maʿrifa* means encompassing knowledge yet Allah cannot be encompassed because He is infinite.

Sufis often differentiate between the concepts of *ʿilm* and *maʿrifa*. The former is a general concept denoting everything that may be learned, including religious sciences. Having *ʿilm* of something means knowing it but does not necessarily mean practising that knowledge. So *ʿilm* does not describe a behavioural state. *Maʿrifa*, on the other hand, refers to experiential, intimate, spiritual knowledge acquired through the state of nearness to Allah. Therefore, *ʿārif* (one who has *maʿrifa*) is a specific and greater description than *ʿālim* (one who has *ʿilm*) for two reasons. First, *maʿrifa* is more profound than *ʿilm*, hence I have translated it as "intimate knowledge". Second, *ʿārif* is someone who has put his knowledge into practice and is near to Allah, which is not necessarily the case for *ʿālim*. So, Sufis use the term *maʿrifa* and its derivatives in the context of talking about states of obeying, worshipping, and being close to Allah. The superiority of *maʿrifa*

---

[1] 188-261 H / 804-875 CE. His grandfather was Zoroastrian before embracing Islam. He was born and died in Bastam, Iran, where his tomb still stands.

over *ʿālim* is clear when both terms are used in the same context. For instance, al-Basṭāmī says, "The *ʿārif* is above what he says, whereas the *ʿālim* is below what he says". This means that the state of the *ʿārif* is greater than what he reveals, whereas the words of the *ʿālim* are greater than his state. He goes on to explain the distinction of the *ʿārif* over the *ʿālim* by his nearness to Allah, "The *ʿārif* watches his Lord, whereas the *ʿālim* watches himself with his knowledge".[1]

> The differing of scholars is a mercy except in the abandonment of means in tawḥīd (*Ṭabaqāt al-ṣūfiyya*, 70).

Ijtihād (personal reasoning) is inevitable for studying the Book of Allah and the Sunna as well as understanding religion and detailing its various matters and rulings. Ijtihād necessarily leads to differences in opinion. This plurality of views is a mercy for Muslims in all religious matters except understanding tawḥīd as requiring avoiding being deceived by the means and relying on the Lord of all means instead. Al-Basṭāmī's words may contain a subtle reference to this ḥadīth, "Differences among my nation is a mercy".[2] Some have rejected the authenticity of this ḥadīth because its chain of narration is unknown. But there is the following similar ḥadīth that is reported on the authority of Ibn ʿAbbās, "Differences among my Companions is a mercy for you".[3]

---

[1] Al-Aṣfahānī, *Ḥilyat al-awliyā*ʾ, vol. 10, 39.

[2] Al-Ghazālī, *Iḥyā*ʾ *ʿulūm al-dīn*, 36.

[3] Al-Bayhaqī, *Al-Madkhal ilā ʿilm al-sunan*, no. 1248.

Sahl Ibn ʿAbd Allah Al-Tustarī[1]

There is nothing in Allah's treasuries greater than tawḥīd (*Ḥilyat al-awliyāʾ*, vol. 10, 196).

The greatest favour that Allah may confer on a servant is tawḥīd.

All creatures eat by Allah yet when worshipping Him they associate others (*Ḥilyat al-awliyāʾ*, vol. 10, 197).

The sustenance of all creatures is from Allah yet they put their trust in other than Him, which is a form of polytheism.

Allah's (exalted is He) being is described by knowledge, cannot be comprehended, and cannot be seen by the eyes in this world. His being is recognised to exist by the truths of faith without being limited, comprehended, or immanent. Eyes will see Him in the hereafter visible and hidden in His kingdom and power. He has blocked the creatures from knowing the essence of His being while guiding them to Himself by His signs. Hearts know Him but intellects cannot reach Him. The believers look at Him with their eyes without comprehending or encompassing Him (*Kashf al-maḥjūb*, 525).

All we know about Allah's being is what He described Himself in the Qur'an, not from intellectual inductions or sensory observations. Faith guides the believer to see Allah through His signs, which are visible everywhere, and Allah bestows on the faithful heart spiritual revelations. The Divine is limitless, incomprehensible, and not present in His creation. In the hereafter,

[1] 200-283 H / 816-897 CE. He came from a place called Tustar in today's Arabistan, Iran. He met Dhū al-Nūn al-Miṣrī and accompanied him.

eyes will see Him but without encompassing Him.

Seeing Allah in the Hereafter has been the subject of disagreement among Muslim scholars. Ahl al-Sunna confirm that Allah will be seen, although they differ over what it exactly means and even accuse a group within of anthropomorphism. Those who deny that Allah will be seen in the Hereafter include the Muʿtazilīs and the Shia.[1]

[1] Ṣabrī, *Ruʾyat Allah*; Al-Ḥamīda, "Ruʾyat Allah taʿālā fī al-ākhira."

Abū Sa'īd Al-Kharrāz[1]

> The first station of one who has acquired knowledge of tawḥīd and applied it is the disappearance of the mention of all things from his heart with only Allah (majestic and exalted is He) being in it (*Al-Luma'*, 53).

Believing in and practising tawḥīd raises the person to spiritual stations, the first of which is that nothing would remain in his heart and it would be occupied only by the remembrance of Allah.

> The first sign of tawḥīd is that the servant would forsake everything and attribute all things to the Ruler so that the ruled one comes to see things, act on them, and control them through the Ruler.

The first sign of tawḥīd is for the servant to cut off all attachments to this world and see everything as made by Allah, existing by His will, and acting by His power.

> He would then hide the ruled from themselves, cause themselves to die as far as they are concerned, and develop them to be His.

In the state of *fanā'* (annihilation), the servant becomes an instrument of the Lord, never ignoring what He commanded him to do or committing what He ordered him not to do. He could then be metaphorically described as no longer existing for he has become annihilated in Allah. This annihilation is not material, so it does not mean the disappearance of the human body of the annihilated servant. Rather, it is in the heart and behaviour as he

[1] N/A-286 H / N/A-899 CE. He lived in Baghdad where he accompanied Sarī al-Saqaṭī, Dhū al-Nūn al-Miṣrī, and Bishr al-Ḥāfī.

acts in total obedience to the Lord. Sayings that reflect the condition of spiritual annihilation are among the most misunderstood and criticised words of Sufi, resulting in falsely and unfairly questioning their tawḥīd.

> This is the first entrance into tawḥīd as it appears through permanency (*Al-Luma*ʿ, 53).

This is the first state of tawḥīd as a permanent intellectual and behavioural state of the servant, not a transient state that he experiences or seeks now and then, for example, when worshipping or reflecting on Allah.

> The people of tawḥīd cut all attachments beside Him, abandon all creatures for Him, forsake comforts, feel strangers with all intimate things, and feel aliens with all familiar things (*Al-Luma*ʿ, 438).

The muwaḥḥids forsake the created for the Creator's sake and love being alone with Him away from all creatures. They prefer worshipping, obeying, and seeking Him over all forms of comfort and luxury. They do not feel intimacy or familiarity with what people find intimate and familiar.

ʿAmru Ibn ʿUthmān Al-Makkī[1]

The reality of our people is tawḥīd. Their alluding (to Him) is polytheism (*Al-Lumaʿ*, 295).

Tawḥīd is the essence of the creed of Sufis. They consider alluding to Him polytheism because that treats Him as if He were a thing, localises Him, or likens Him when He is not a thing and is unlike anything.

He read these verses, "Successful are the believers, who are submissive in their prayers" (al-Muʾminūn 23:1-2), then he said, "Anything other than Allah that occurs in the heart is vain". He then read these two verses, "Those are the inheritors, who will inherit paradise in which they will stay forever" (al-Muʾminūn 23:10-11) (*Al-Lumaʿ*, 112).

There should be nothing in the heart other than Allah.

Anything that your heart imagines, appears in the flow of your thought, or occurs to your heart—whether a splendour or brilliance, familiarity or radiance, beauty or ugliness, light or ghost, or person or apparition—Allah (exalted is He) is far from all of it. He is greater, exalted, and more illustrious. Have you not heard His (exalted is He) words, "There is nothing like Him, and He is the hearing, the seeing" (al-Shūrāʾ 42:11) and "He has not begotten and He has not been begotten, and there has never been one equal to Him" (al-Ikhlāṣ 112:3-4) (*Al-*

---

[1] N/A-291 H / N/A-904 CE. He lived and died in Baghdad. He accompanied Abū Saʿīd Al-Kharrāz. He was a scholar of the sources of jurisprudence and had works on Sufism.

*Luma*ʿ, 164).

Allah is unlike anything, physical or non-physical, existent or hypothetical.

Ibrāhīm Ibn Aḥmad Al-Khawwāṣ[1]

[Tawḥīd by the elect] is to see Allah alone by discarding any effects anything may have on them:

The elite's tawḥīd is to not let a created thing have any effect on them, thus seeing nothing and no one other than Him.

If the Sea of China were between us,
I would see that as a mirage that leaves no trace (*Al-Luma'*, 432).

In this poetry, a lover says to his beloved that if they were separated by a barrier as vast as the Sea of China, his dedication to his beloved would make him see the sea as no more than a traceless mirage, thus not occupying him away from his beloved or stopping him from seeking him. This is the situation of the muwaḥḥid in his love for the Wāḥid.

[1] N/A-291 H / N/A-904 CE. He was born in Samarra, Iraq, but lived in Rayy, Iran, and died in the Rayy mosque. Many sayings on trust, renunciation, and other subjects have been attributed to him.

Abū Al-Ḥusayn Al-Nūrī[1]

A man asked him, "What is the proof of Allah?" He replied, "Allah". The enquirer asked, "What is the intellect then?" He replied, "The intellect is incompetent and what is incompetent can only refer to what is incompetent like it" (*Al-Taʿarruf*, 37).

The intellect is not the source of the proof of Allah because it is limited, so it cannot provide proof of Allah, whose ability is infinite. The intellect's proof of Allah is Allah who made Himself known to the intellect through His revelation to His Messengers.

The people of religion are stopped, the people of tawḥīd continue to move, the people of content rest, and the people of devotion feel bewildered. When the Real One appears, every obscuring and concealing thing disappears (*Ṭabaqāt al-ṣūfiyya*, 137).

Some people seek a limited amount of religion, those who seek tawḥīd never stop seeking closeness to Him, those who are content by whatever He decreed are in a state of comfort and peace, and those who have shunned creatures and completely dedicated themselves to Allah experience amazing spiritual and supernatural wonders. Allah's manifestation in the heart of a servant makes him experience that Allah is the only real existing one and everything else exists because of and by Him, so hidden spiritual truths and secrets are revealed to him.

Tawḥīd is when every thought alludes to Allah (exalted

---

[1] N/A-295 H / N/A-908 CE. His title is drived from the city of Nūr, between Bukhārā and Samarkand, Uzbekistan, or from *nūr* (light) on his face. He accompanied Sarī al-Saqaṭī. His tomb is in al-Aʿẓamiyya, Baghdad, Iraq.

> is He) without it being mixed with any thoughts of likening Him to something else (*Al-Risāla al-qushayriyya*, 32).

Tawḥīd is a state in which everything that occurs to the person reminds him of Allah, without those thoughts being corrupted by those that liken Him to other things.

Al-Junayd Al-Baghdādī[1]

Know that the beginning of worshipping Allah (majestic and exalted is He) is knowing Him, and the origin of knowing Allah is affirming His oneness. The way to affirm His oneness is to deny describing Him in terms of condition, time, and space. It is through Him that it was possible to be guided to Him. The cause of being guided to Him is His enablement, for by His enablement, His oneness is affirmed, and by affirming His oneness, believing in Him takes place (*Rasāʾil al-Junayd*, 58).

Knowing Allah means practising tawḥīd, and tawḥīd is the foundation of worshipping Him, so He cannot be properly worshipped without tawḥīd. The latter means denying that he has a condition, exists in a space, or is time-bound. Tawḥīd cannot happen without His guidance, "And whomsoever Allah guides, he is rightly guided" (al-ʾIsrāʾ 17:97).

Know that creatures find guidance by having truthfulness and exerting efforts to establish the requirements of each state. Each state would then lead the creature to another until they lead him to the reality of outward servanthood, which is abandoning choice and

[1] 215-298- H / 831-911 CE. He is one of the best known Sufis. He was born and lived in Baghdad. He accompanied his uncle, Sarī al-Saqaṭī, and al-Ḥārith al-Muḥāsibī, and he learned jurisprudence from Abū Thawr al-Kalbī al-Baghdādī. He showed signs of wisdom while a small child. For example, once Sarī asked him about the meaning of gratefulness, so he replied, "That you do not disobey Allah with His favours". One indication of his high status is that he is called *Sayyid al-Ṭāʾifa* (the Master of the Group), meaning the group of Sufis, *Tāj al-ʿĀrifīn* (the Crown of the Intimate Knowers), and other titles. He is buried in Baghdad in a cemetery that is named after him, next to Sarī al-Saqaṭī.

> being satisfied with His action (*Rasā'il al-Junayd*, 59-60).

Truthfulness, good works, and performing what each spiritual state requires progress the person from one state to another until his servanthood is realised. The latter means the disappearance of his will and being in total submission to Allah's decree.

> Know that you are veiled from you by you. You do not reach Him by you but you reach Him by Him. Because when He informed you about reaching Him, He called on you to seek Him, so you did. You are seeking and exerting efforts to get what you want. You are veiled until you resort to Him in what you seek. Thus, He becomes your pillar and support in your seeking, in the intensity of your seeking, in discharging the duties of what He chose for you of the knowledge of seeking, in fulfilling the conditions He set for you concerning it, and in looking after what He left to you to take care of for your benefit.

Drawing near to Allah requires acknowledging that it is He who called on the servant to seek Him, showed him the way to Him, and enabled him to fulfil the requirements of drawing near to Him.

> He protected you from yourself so that He would make you attain your subsistence through your annihilation for you have reached your destination. You would subsist through His subsistence because the tawḥīd of the muwaḥḥid subsists by the subsistence of the Wāḥid, even when the muwaḥḥid experiences annihilation. Then, you become yourself by being without yourself and you subsist through annihilation (*Rasā'il al-Junayd*, 60).

A person's annihilation of himself for Allah to become a perfect servant is the highest degree of tawḥīd. This annihilation is the true subsistence because it is annihilation for the Subsistent One.

Know that there are three kinds of people: a journeying seeker, one who has arrived and stopped at the door, and one who is staying inside.

As for the seeker of Allah (majestic and exalted is He), he moves towards Him guided by the signs of outward knowledge, dealing with Allah (majestic and exalted is He) with the hard work of his outward.

The one who arrives at the door and stops there discerns the positions of His drawing him near, by the signs of purifying his inward and showering him with benefits. He deals with Allah (majestic and exalted is He) with his inward.

The one who is wholly inside stands before Him, does not see anyone other than Him, is attentive to His allusion to him, and promptly obeys what his Master commands him. This is the state of the muwaḥḥid of Allah (majestic and exalted is He) (*Rasāʾil al-Junayd*, 61).

The first believer purifies his inward by applying Sharīʿa in full, so he is in a continuous state of drawing near to Allah. The second combines following Sharīʿa with purifying his heart, so he arrives at the door of the divine presence but does not enter inside because he still sees other than Allah. As for the third believer, he combines applying Sharīʿa and purifying his heart with abandoning his will and being annihilated in his Lord, so Allah admits him to the place of nearness. This is the perfect tawḥīd.

Know that tawḥīd by creatures occurs in four forms: one is the tawḥīd of ordinary people, another is the tawḥīd of the people of outward knowledge, and the other two are the tawḥīd of the elect who have intimate knowledge.

> The tawḥīd of ordinary people is confessing Oneness by not seeing any lords, peers, opposites, forms, and likes (for Him), and not being moved by the causes of desire in and fear of anyone other than Him. It is truly realised in the deeds by the subsistence of the confession.

The minimal requirement of tawḥīd is exaltating Allah over everything in thoughts and words. As long as the servant maintains this, tawḥīd shows in his actions, even though it is admixed with wanting and fearing other than Allah.

> The tawḥīd of the people of the truths of the knowledge of the outward is confessing Oneness by not seeing any lords, peers, forms, and likes (for Him), combined with establishing the commandments and refraining from the prohibitions outwardly. This is the result of them having desire, fear, hope, and wishes (with respect to Allah). This is realised in the deeds because of the truthfulness of the confession.

This is the tawḥīd of the person who applies Sharīʿa, so it shows in his actions always, hence it is greater than that of the ordinary people.

> As for the first type of tawḥīd by one of the elect, it is confessing Oneness by not seeing those things anymore, combined with establishing the commandments, outwardly and inwardly, by removing the causes of desire in and fear of anyone other than Him. This is the result of compliance, having evidence from the Real One and evidence from the call and the response.

This tawḥīd of the elect is greater than that of the people of the outward because it is combined with the vanishing of desiring or fearing anyone other than Allah and being supported by spiritual proofs of Allah's call to the servant to affirm His oneness and his answering it.

> The second type of tawḥīd by one of the elect is when the person becomes an apparition standing in His presence, without a third with them. He becomes subject to the workings of His management of affairs through the decrees of His power in the stormy waters of the seas of affirming His oneness. He does this by annihilation and by unawareness of the call of the Real One and his responding to Him, to exist instead by the truths of His oneness in the reality of His nearness, by the loss of his senses and motion as the Real One would use him as He wills. This represents the servant's return to his very beginning, becoming as he was before he came into being. The evidence of this is in the words of Allah (majestic and exalted is He), "And when your Lord took from the children of Adam—from their loins—their descendants and made them testify of themselves, 'Am I not your Lord?' They said, 'Yes, we have testified'" (al-Aʿrāf 7:172). This is what and how he was before he came into being. Was it other than the pure, good, sacred souls who answered by affirming the prevailing power and full will, that he is now as he was before he came into being? This is the ultimate goal of the tawḥīd of the Wāḥid by the muwaḥḥid, which is letting go of his self (*Rasāʾil al-Junayd*, 61-62).

The second of the two types of the tawḥīd of the elect, which is the greatest form of tawḥīd, includes all that is in the first type. It excels over it by the servant attaining the state of annihilation in Allah, becoming an instrument in His hand, with no will of his own. This way, he realises his earlier testimony to the lordship of

Allah and his own servanthood. Most scholars say that the question, "Am I not your Lord?", was posed when Allah created Adam, which is when He made his progeny from his loin. The interpretation that I am inclined towards makes the subject of the question the sperm in the loin of the man, and the timing of the question is when Allah creates a human being out of it.[1]

The question reveals that Allah made tawḥīd an intrinsic part of the nature of the human being, as in the following verse, "The innate nature (*fiṭra*) in which Allah has created man" (al-Rūm 30:30). The Prophet (PBUH) said, "Every child is born with that innate nature (of Islam), so it is his parents who make him a Jew, Christian, or Magi".[2] When his intellectual faculties develop, he exercises his will in choosing to confirm or contravene his nature, "So whoever wills, let him believe; and whoever wills, let him disbelieve" (al-Kahf 18:29).

> Tawḥīd is exiting the narrowness of the time-bound traces to the spaciousness of the domain of eternity (*Al-Luma'*, 49).

Tawḥīd is to stop being occupied with the world of creatures, which is limited in time and space, to only reflect on the limitless Creator.

> [Tawḥīd is] a reality in which all traces vanish and all sciences disappear while Allah (exalted is He) remains as He has been from eternity (*Al-Luma'*, 49).

In tawḥīd, things appear as signs pointing to the Creator, and the failure of sciences to know Allah becomes clear, as He remains

---

[1] One classical exegetical work that discusses this matter in detail is Fakhr al-Dīn al-Rāzī's *Al-Tafsīr al-kabīr*. Al-Rāzī thinks that the two interpretations can be reconciled.

[2] Muslim, *Al-Ṣaḥīḥ*, 2658.

incomprehensible as He has been from eternity.

> [Tawḥīd] is the confirmation of the uniqueness of the Wāḥid by the realisation of His oneness by the perfection of His singularity. This is achieved by acknowledging that He is the One who "has not begotten and has not been begotten" (al-Ikhlāṣ 112:3); denying that He has opposites, peers, or likes; rejecting that there is anyone and anything that is worthy of worship other than Him; not likening Him to anything else; not assigning a condition to Him; not imagining Him; not having a representation of Him; and accepting that He is one deity, self-sufficient, alone, as stated in this verse, "There is nothing like Him, and He is the hearing, the seeing" (al-Shūrā 42:11) (*Al-Luma'*, 49).

Tawḥīd is confessing that His oneness is unique by denying that He has children or parents; that He has an opposite, peer, or anyone or anything that resembles Him in any way; and the divinity of anyone else that is worshipped; not likening Him to anyone; not thinking of the condition of His existence; and not imagining Him. He is unique in His oneness and is in need of no one. No one resembles Him in being, attributes, or actions, as He described Himself in verses 112:3 and 42:11.

> [Muwaḥḥids] exist without presence and depart without separation (*Al-Luma'*, 432).

The muwaḥḥid is among the creatures as far as his body is concerned, but he is isolated from them with respect to his heart because he is always occupied with his Lord. He is with the creatures without being with them and he is separated from them without being away from them.

> The servant does not attain the reality of intimate knowledge and purity of tawḥīd until he traverses through

the states and stations[1] (*Al-Luma'*, 436).

The servant does not attain the most sublime truths nor does his tawḥīd become complete until he reaches the various spiritual ranks and tastes its fruits of revelation.

> You will not be a real servant to Him if something other than Him has enslaved you. You will not achieve total freedom if something is still lacking in your servanthood to Him. If you are a servant to Him alone, you are free of everything else (*Ṭabaqāt al-ṣūfiyya*, 131).

The person cannot be a true servant of Allah while he is enslaved by something. He cannot be free of servanthood to other than Allah until He is a servant to Him alone. Servanthood to Allah means freedom from others.

> Tawḥīd is to know and confess that Allah is alone in His firstness and eternity, there is no one else with Him, and no one can perform His action and His actions that He kept for Himself (*Ḥilyat al-awliyā'*, vol. 10, 256).

Tawḥīd is the realisation of the intellect and belief of the heart that preexistence and eternity are unique to Allah, for "He is the First and the Last" (al-Ḥadīd 57:3). No one has similar powers and no one performs the actions of Lordship other than Him for there is no other Lord.

> The first requirement of the wisdom that the servant needs is knowing who made what is made and how what is originated was originated. This way he would know how to distinguish the Creator from the created and the Ancient from the originated. He would submit to His call

[1] According to Sufis, a "state" is a temporary spiritual experience whereas a "station" is an ongoing spiritual state and rank.

> and acknowledge the necessity of obeying Him. Whoever does not know his owner would not attribute ownership to its rightful proprietor (*Al-Risāla al-qushayriyya*, 26).

The first requirement of wisdom is knowing there is only one ancient Creator and that everything else has a beginning in time and is originated by Him, so the creature would obey and submit to the Creator. One's failure to do that amounts to denying that He is his Creator, failing to affirm His oneness, and not realising his servanthood.

> How could He who is likeless and peerless connect with he who has a like and a peer? Impossible! This is a bizarre belief! There could only be subtle actions of the Subtle One where there is no contact, no illusion, and no encompassing (Him) other than by the allusion of certitude and realisation of faith (*Al-Risāla al-qushayriyya*, 33).

No one and nothing can physically connect to Allah because He is unique, with no likes or peers. Allah's drawing a servant near to Him is subtle and intangible. It does not involve reaching Him physically, imagining him in a particular shape, or encompassing Him intellectually or by imagination. It is a matter based on faith and certitude.

> Trust (in Allah) is an action of the heart and tawḥīd is a speech of the heart (*Al-Risāla al-qushayriyya*, 36).

Tawḥīd is a verbal declaration whose proof is the muwaḥḥid's trust in Allah.

> The Real One alone knows the unseen. He knows what was, what will be, and what will not be, meaning how it would be were it to be (*Al-Risāla al-qushayriyya*, 36).

Allah alone knows what happened, will happen, and will not

happen.

> The noblest and loftiest assembly is sitting with the mind in the field of tawḥīd (*Al-Risāla al-qushayriyya*, 36).

The foremost conference is the dedication to thinking of the oneness of Allah.

> When the intellects of sensible people reach the furthest limits of tawḥīd, they reach a state of bewilderment (*Al-Risāla al-qushayriyya*, 493).

Tawḥīd is denying anything familiar, known, or even imagined about the reality of the One. Therefore, the deeper a sound intellect reflects on tawḥīd, the greater its perplexity about the Wāḥid.

> Tawḥīd that is unique to Sufis is distinguishing ancientness from being originated, leaving one's homeland, giving up what one loves, abandoning what is known and unknown, and having the Real One (glory be to Him) replace all (*Al-Risāla al-qushayriyya*, 495-496).

Sufis are unique in their tawḥīd in combining the following: attributing ancientness to Him alone because everything else came into being at some point, forsaking everything for His sake so that He is the only companion, turning away from everything that occupies the heart away from Him, abandoning any knowledge that does not bring the person closer to Him, and making Him one's only concern and occupation.

> The knowledge of tawḥīd rolled up its carpet twenty years ago, and people only talk about its edges (*Al-Risāla al-qushayriyya*, 496).

Past scholars spoke in detail about tawḥīd. Any new statements about it would only be minor, secondary additions. The use of the number "twenty" may be allegorical referring to all past scholars; otherwise, it indicates that speaking about tawḥīd reached its furthest limits at the hands of the scholars of the generation immediately before that of al-Junayd.

> The noblest saying about tawḥīd is these words of Abū Bakr al-Ṣiddīq (may Allah be satisfied with him), "Glory be to Him who did not give His creatures a way to know Him other than by the inability to know Him" (*Kashf al-maḥjūb*, 525).

There is no way to know Allah by the intellect or imagination. He is known only as He described Himself. Denying this epistemological inability leads to having wrong thoughts about Him.

Ruwaym Ibn Aḥmad Al-Baghdādī[1]

Tawḥīd means the eradication of all the effects of human nature and the exaltation of divinity (*Al-Luma*ʿ, 51).

Tawḥīd is the annihilation of the self, so the person becomes an instrument in Allah's hand, combined with the exaltation of the Creator over everything.

He was asked about when a servant confirms his servanthood, so he said, "When he surrenders his control from himself to his Lord, disowns his own ability and power, and realises that all is His and by Him" (*Al-Luma*ʿ, 51).

Servanthood becomes true when the servant surrenders to his Lord, denies that he has power over anything, and acknowledges that Allah owns everything and is the Originator of everything that comes into being and happens.

[1] N/A-303 H / N/A-916 CE. He was a judge, Qur'an reciter, and jurist. He accompanied al-Junayd al-Baghdādī. He died in Baghdad.

Yūsuf Ibn Al-Ḥusayn Al-Rāzī[1]

Whoever falls in the seas of tawḥīd would only grow more thirsty with time (*Al-Risāla al-qushayriyya*, 496).

Tawḥīd is a continuous state whose delight one can never have enough of and in which he never stops seeking more nearness to Allah.

[1] N/A-304 H / N/A-917 CE. He was a scholar and an author. He accompanied Dhū al-Nūn al-Miṣrī and traveled with Abū Sa'īd Al-Kharrāz on some of his journeys.

Aḥmad Abū ʿAbd Allah Ibn Al-Jallāʾ[1]

Whoever sees praise and disapproval as equal is an ascetic. Whoever performs the obligatory acts of worship as soon as they are due is a worshipper. Whoever sees all actions from Allah (majestic and exalted is He) is a muwaḥḥid (*Ṭabaqāt al-ṣūfiyya*, 146).

The ascetic is not one who renunciates only the pleasure of this world but one who also does not feel pleased when praised or saddened when blamed. His total focus is on the Creator and he is completely disinterested in the creatures. The worshipper is not one who only performs the obligatory acts of worship but one who also does so as soon as they become due. By giving them priority over anything else, he applies these words of Allah Almighty, "And I did not create the jinn and mankind except to worship Me" (al-Ḍāriyāt 51:56). As for the muwaḥḥid, he is one who sees Allah as the source of all happenings regardless of their apparent causes.

[1] N/A-306 H / N/A-919 CE. He was a judge and Shāfiʿī jurist. He is credited with the spreading of the Shāfiʿī school of thought in Baghdad. He accompanied Dhū al-Nūn al-Miṣrī. He died in Damascus.

ʿAlī Ibn Sahl Al-Aṣbahānī[1]

I see people pleased with aggrandising themselves and refining their words so much so that they have no time for the One who honoured them by making them a special kind of creation and allowed their tongues to affirm His oneness (*Ṭabaqāt al-ṣūfiyya*, 189).

Most people are too busy self-ennobling and polishing their words to remember Allah, who honoured them with a unique nature among His creatures and enabled them to proclaim His oneness.

He was asked about the true nature of tawḥīd, so he said, "It is close to conjectures but remote from truths". He went on to quote the following poetry by someone:

So I said to my companions, like the sun, its light
is near, but it is too far to reach (*Ṭabaqāt al-ṣūfiyya*, 189).

What a person can know about the true nature of tawḥīd is closer to guessing than the truth because Allah is incomprehensible.

[1] N/A-307 H / N/A-920 CE. He is from Isfahan, Iran. He corresponded with al-Junayd al-Baghdādī.

Al-Ḥusayn Ibn Manṣūr Al-Ḥallāj[1]

O You who has intoxicated me with His love and has confounded me in the fields of His nearness! You are alone in ancientness and the only One in being on the seat of truthfulness. You stand in justice, not physically. Your remoteness is by not mixing with things, not by being in isolation. Your presence is in knowledge, not by moving, and Your absence is by veiling, not travelling.

"Standing", "nearness" and "remoteness", and "presence" and "absence" are used symbolically when referring to Allah, not with their meanings when used for creatures.

There is nothing above You so it would overshadow You, and there is nothing below You so it would raise You. There is nothing in front of You so it would make You try to catch it, and there is nothing behind You so it would reach You.

Allah is exalted over anthropomorphism, being likened, being imagined, and being associated with a location.

I ask You by the sanctity of these accepted tombs and lofty ranks[2] that You do not return me to me after You

---

[1] 244-309 H / 859-922 CE. He accompanied Sahl al-Tustarī, Abū al-Ḥusayn al-Nūrī, and al-Junayd al-Baghdādī. Some denounced him as a disbeliever due to misunderstanding some of his utterances that are open to serious misinterpretation, whereas others exonerated him. He was imprisoned by the Abbasid caliph Ja'far al-Muqtadir bi-Llah and was later killed during the time of his minister Ḥāmid Ibn al-'Abbās. His words here clearly show the purity of his tawḥīd and the falsehood of the charges against him.

[2] "Accepted tombs" refers to the graves of righteous people, such as Aḥmad Ibn Ḥanbal (164-241 H / 780-855 CE), and "lofty ranks" to their high statuses.

have snatched me from me, and that You do not make me see myself after You have veiled it from me (*Akhbār al-Ḥallāj*, 67).

Al-Ḥallāj was heard saying this prayer while weeping at the grave of Aḥmad Ibn Ḥanbal. Invoking the status of righteous people, Al-Ḥallāj prayed to Allah to keep him annihilated in Him away from himself.

Anyone who thinks that divinity mixes with humanity or that humanity mixes with divinity commits disbelief. For Allah (exalted is He) is unique in His being and attributes, unlike the beings and attributes of the creatures. He does not resemble them in any aspect and they do not resemble Him in anything. How could any similarity between what is ancient and what is originated be conceived? Anyone who claims that the Creator is in a place, is on a place, is linked to a place, could be conceptualised, could be conceived in the imagination, or could be described and characterised commits polytheism (*Akhbār al-Ḥallāj*, 77).

Thinking that any overlap between the divinity of the Creator and the humanity of the human being is possible is disbelief. There is no similarity whatsoever between the ancient Creator and the creatures, who are all originated. Any mental depiction or imagining of Allah is polytheism.

Know that Allah creates all causes but He is not a cause. How can be a cause He who was when there was nothing, who created from nothing, and who is now as He was when there was nothing? Glorified and exalted is He, had He been a cause, He would have had a connection, and had He had a connection, He would not have been perfect.

> Exalted be to Allah over what the wrongdoers claim, a great exaltation[1] (*Al-Tajalliyāt al-ilāhiyya*, 138–139).

Allah is the Creator of everything and the Originator of all causes but He is not a cause. Had He been a cause, He would have been connected to His creation so He would have been imperfect.

> It is sufficiently gratifying for the one in ecstasy to not see other than the Wāḥid[2] (*Al-Luma'*, 378, 425).

It is enough satisfaction for the lover to not see other than his one Beloved. The true muwaḥḥid does not see in the variety of creatures other than the power and fashioning of the One Creator, Allah.

> It is not proper for someone who sees or mentions any single thing to say, "I have known the One by whom all single things were created" (*Ṭabaqāt al-ṣūfiyya*, 238).

Knowing the one Creator requires seeing everything as a creature that points to its Creator. The true muwaḥḥid does not see the various creatures other than signs pointing to the One Creator, Allah.

> The person who is intoxicated by the lights of tawḥīd is veiled by them from expressions of the abandonment of means. Furthermore, the person who is intoxicated by the lights of the abandonment of means speaks out the truths of tawḥīd because only an intoxicated person utters any concealed thing (*Ṭabaqāt al-ṣūfiyya*, 239).

---

[1] Muḥyī al-Dīn Ibn 'Arabī says that al-Ḥallāj told him these words in a spiritual encounter with him.

[2] Al-Ḥallāj is said to have uttered this after he was taken out of prison to be executed, so it was among his last words.

Most muwaḥḥids do not discard the means but some are inebriated by tawḥīd to the point of not seeing other than the Lord of the means. If annihilation in Allah intoxicates their senses and intellects and they describe this special spiritual state that the language cannot accurately describe, some of their words would sound, to those who do not understand this station, as if lacking in exalting Allah. Examples of these include al-Ḥallāj's utterances, "I am the Real One" and "There is nothing in this robe other than Allah".

> Consider everything to have originated at some point because ancientness is His alone. Anything that appears in corporeal form is subject to accidents. Anything that is made whole by a means, the power of this means is what holds it together. Anything that is formed at a certain time is disbanded at another time. Anything that is supported by something else is subject to necessities. Anything that is accessible to the imagination can be given an image. Anything that is contained in a place has a whereabouts. Anything that has a type is made so by a fashioner.

Everything other than Allah is originated, as He alone is ancient. Anything that has a physical body is subject to change; anything that depends on something else, the continuation of its existence is subject to the existence of that cause; anything that comes into existence at a certain time is bound to cease to exist at another time; anything that may be imagined can be pictured; anything that may be contained somewhere has a location to refer to; and anything that has a type is subject to change by the laws of the type maker. None of these characteristics apply to Allah Almighty.

> Glory be to Him! There is nothing above Him and nothing below Him. He does not have a limit nor is anything with Him. There is no behindness to Him nor is

> there frontness. No beforeness caused Him to appear nor will there be afterness that causes Him to perish. He is not made of parts, He did not appear at a certain time, and He does not miss anything.

Allah is not identified or limited by directions. There is no time in which He was not or will not be extant. He is not subject to increase or decrease.

> His attribute is indescribable, His action has no cause, and His existence has no end in time. He is exalted over the conditions of His creatures. None of His creatures mixes with Him, and His actions do not involve interactions. He differs from His creatures by His ancientness and they differ from Him by their origination.

He is not describable with familiar attributes. There is no cause for His action other than His will. There is no end to His existence because He is eternal. Descriptions of His creatures do not apply to Him. He does not mix with them nor does He interact with them. He is distinct from His creatures by His ancientness, and they are distinct from Him by each of them having appeared at some point in time.

> If you say "when", that would mean that time existed before Him. If you say *Hū* (He), the *H* and *ū* are both created by Him. If you say "where", that would mean that space existed before Him.

He cannot be referred to with "when" and "where" because He created space and time, so He existed before them and is outside them. Everything is created by Him, even the two letters of the word *Hū* (He), which refers to Him.

> The letters are His signs, His existence is the

confirmation of Him, knowing Him is affirming His oneness, and affirming His oneness is distinguishing Him from His creatures. Whatever the imagination conceives about Him, He is different from that. How could something originated by Him dwell in Him? How could something created by Him return to Him? The eyes cannot see Him and conjectures cannot guess Him. Nearness to Him is His bestowal of honour and remoteness from Him is His infliction of humiliation. His elevation is without climbing and His coming is without moving, "He is the First and the Last and the Manifest and the Hidden" (al-Ḥadīd 57:3), He is the close and the remote who "there is nothing like Him, and He is the hearing, the seeing" (al-Shūrā 42:11)[1] (*Al-Risāla al-qushayriyya*, 27-28).

The letters of His revelations are signs pointing to Him. His existence is the proof of Him. Knowing Him truly means to affirm His Oneness, which in turn means distinguishing Him from His creation and exalting Him over what may be imagined. He is inaccessible to the eyes and conjectures. He is not describable by expressions of movement. He is the first before anything ever existed, and He is the last after everything is gone. He is more visible than everything because everything He creates points to Him. He is more hidden than everything because no sense or faculty can reach Him. He is infinitely close to His creatures yet they are immeasurably far from Him. He is without a like, and nothing is hidden from Him.

The person who knows the truth of tawḥīd would not

---

[1] Ibn Taymiyya quoted this relatively long saying of al-Ḥallāj in full and commented on it in detail. Although he objected to some of it, among what he agreed with is what he saw as refutation of the doctrine of *ittiḥād* and *ḥulūl*, Ibn Taymiyya, *Al-Istiqāma,* vol. 1, 117-139.

> ask "why" and "how" (*Al-Risāla al-qushayriyya*, 36).

The true muwaḥḥid does not ask why and how something happened because he knows that the answer to both questions is the divine will.

> [Allah is] the originating cause of all creatures while He has no cause of origination Himself (*Al-Risāla al-qushayriyya*, 496).

Allah is the cause of the existence of everything but there is no cause for His existence.

> The first step in tawḥīd is the annihilation of not seeing other than Him (*Kashf al-maḥjūb*, 522).

The first station of tawḥīd is the annihilation in which the servant wouldn't see anything other than the One, Allah.

Aḥmad Ibn ʿAṭāʾ Al-Baghdādī al-Ādamī[1]

The sign of true tawḥīd is forgetting tawḥīd. Genuine tawḥīd is when the person who practises it is one (*Al-Lumaʿ*, 55).

Tawḥīd is truthful when it is a permanent, not temporary, state. The sign of this is the person's unawareness of being in that state. The muwaḥḥid is in one continuous state of tawḥīd.

There are two types of knowledge: real knowledge and true knowledge. Real knowledge is to know His oneness through His names and attributes that He made known to creatures. True knowledge, on the other hand, is impossible because of the self-sufficiency and realisation of Lordship, for He said, "and they do not encompass Him in knowledge" (Ṭāhā 20:110) (*Al-Lumaʿ*, 56).

Allah made His creatures know Him by the revelation of His names and attributes. Other than that, His reality is inaccessible to any creature because it is impossible for a servant to know the Lord.

The intellect is an instrument for servanthood, not for overseeing the Lordship (*Al-Taʿarruf*, 37).

The intellect is a tool for realising servanthood, not for encompassing the reality of Allah's Lordship.

Everything you enquire about you should seek it in the

---

[1] N/A-309 H / N/A-922 CE. He accompanied al-Junayd al-Baghdādī. The minister Ḥāmid Ibn al-ʿAbbās asked him about his view of al-Ḥallāj to see whether he would condemn him, but he told him that he should instead reflect on the properties he confiscated and the blood he shed. The angry minister had Ibn ʿAṭāʾ's teeth extracted, causing his death two weeks later.

> victorious place of knowledge. If you do not find it there, look for it in the arena of wisdom. If you do not find it there either, then measure it by tawḥīd. If you do not find it in any of these three, then strike the face of Satan with it (*Al-Risāla al-qushayriyya*, 97).

Anything that is not supported by knowledge, is not testified to by wisdom, or does not point to the oneness of Allah is a delusion from Satan that should be avoided.

Abū Muḥammad Al-Jurayrī[1]

If someone approaches the knowledge of tawḥīd without proof from it, the foot of vanity would make him slip and fall into a deadly abyss (*Al-Luma'*, 444).

Speaking about tawḥīd without knowledge of it is a conceit that makes the person susceptible to committing fatal mistakes.

The knowledge of tawḥīd does not have other than the tongue of tawḥīd (*Al-Risāla al-qushayriyya*, 493).

The knowledge of tawḥīd is entirely based on Allah's revealed words about it. Any *ijtihād* about it must be confined to interpreting the Qur'anic revelation.

[1] N/A- 311 H / N/A-924 CE. He accompanied Sarī al-Saqaṭī, Sahl al-Tustarī, and al-Junayd al-Baghdādī.

Abū Al-Ḥusayn Al-Warrāq Al-Naysābūrī[1]

Certitude is a fruit of tawḥīd. Anyone whose tawḥīd is pure, his certitude is also pure (*Ṭabaqāt al-ṣūfiyya*, 230).

If a person's tawḥīd was not complete, his belief would not reach certainty.

[1] N/A-319 H / N/A-931 CE. He was from the city of Neyshabur of the Khorasan province, in the northeast of Iran. He was a scholar of Sharī'a.

Abū Bakr Al-Wāṣiṭī[1]

The muwaḥḥid sees only pure Lordship that is in charge of total servanthood, which includes dealing with the decrees and accepting one's fortunes (*Ṭabaqāt al-ṣūfiyya*, 233).

Perfect tawḥīd is seeing Allah as the one Lord who has full power and seeing one's self as a servant whose only option is to fully surrender to the will of his Lord. This includes believing that everything is decreed by Allah and that the servant would only get what Allah allocated to him.

The souls and bodies were brought into being and made to appear by Allah, not by themselves. Similarly, thoughts and movements were brought into being by Allah, not by themselves, because movements and thoughts are properties of the bodies and souls (*Al-Risāla al-qushayriyya*, 30-31).

The souls and bodies are all created by Allah and their continued existence is by His will. The same is true of everything that results from them. Allah is the creator of the essences of things and all incidents that result from them, whether physical, such as movements, or mental, such as thoughts.

Belief and disbelief and this world and the hereafter are from Allah, to Allah, by Allah, and Allah's. From Allah is their creation and initiation, to Allah is their return and end, by Allah is their endurance and perishment, and to

---

[1] N/A-320 H / N/A-932 CE. He came from Fergana in today's Uzbekistan. He visited Baghdad and accompanied Abū al-Ḥusayn al-Nūrī and al-Junayd al-Baghdādī. He left Baghdad to live in Khorasan.

> Allah belongs their ownership and creation (*Al-Risāla al-qushayriyya*, 31).

Perfect tawḥīd is to believe that everything is from Allah and for Allah even though the causes and routes are numerous and diverse.

> Truthfulness is having sound tawḥīd and following the straight path (*Al-Risāla al-qushayriyya*, 367).

Truthfulness is combining proper tawḥīd with diligently seeking Allah, so truthfulness is combining belief and good deeds.

> Allah did not create anything more honourable than the soul (*Al-Risāla al-qushayriyya*, 36).

Even the soul, which is the most honourable of Allah's creation, is originated, so everything must be originated. Only Allah is ancient.

Muḥammad Ibn ʿAlī Al-Tirmidhī[1]

Allah called the muwaḥḥids to the five prayers as a mercy from Him to them. He prepared for them in the prayers various hospitalities so that the servant would acquire by every word and action something of His favours. Actions are like foods and words are like drinks, as prayers are the wedding of the muwaḥḥids (*Ṭabaqāt al-ṣūfiyya*, 176).

The five daily prayers are among the rites and expressions of tawḥīd. Allah endowed them with so many rewards and spiritual benefits for the muwaḥḥid to avail of with every word he utters and movement he makes.

---

[1] N/A-320 H / N/A-932 CE. He was born in Termez, in today's Uzbekistan, hence he was also known as al-Ḥakīm al-Tirmidhī. He was expelled from Termez because of his book *Khatm al-wilāya wa ʿilal al-sharīʿa* (The Seal of Sainthood and the Causes of Sharīʿa), as he was wrongly accused of believing that the status of walī is higher than that of prophet. He visited Neyshabur, whose Shaikhs quoted him.

Abū ʿAlī Al-Jūzjānī[1]

The following three things are foundations of tawḥīd: fear, hope, and love. The increase of fear of having a plentitude of sins comes from seeing the warning (of hell), the increase of hope of doing good stems from seeing the promise (of paradise), and the increase of love for the abundance of remembrance comes from seeing the favours (of Allah).

Fearing Allah's punishment, hoping for His favours, and loving Him confirm the servant's tawḥīd.

The fearful person never stops running away, the hopeful person never stops seeking more, and the lover never stops mentioning the Beloved.

The fearful person always runs away from sins, the hopeful person continues to seek good works and nearness to Allah, and the lover always remembers his Beloved because he is in continuous awareness of His favours.

Fear is a shining fire, hope is an illuminating light, and love is the light of all lights (*Ṭabaqāt al-ṣūfiyya*, 197).

Fear is a light of guidance, hope is a light that illuminates the path to Allah, and love is the source of all lights that guide to Him.

---

[1] His dates of birth and death are unknown but Abū ʿAbd al-Raḥmān al-Sulamī says in *Ṭabaqāt al-ṣūfiyya* that he accompanied Muḥammad Ibn ʿAlī al-Tirmidhī (d. 320/932 CE) and was close to him in age. He was from Khorasan. He is said to have written several books.

Abū ʿAlī Al-Rūdhabārī[1]

Tawḥīd is the uprightness of the heart by rejecting the denial of the ancientness of Allah's names and attributes and repudiating likening Him to anything. Tawḥīd in one statement is this, "Whatever the imagination and thoughts conceive, Allah (glorified is He) is different from it", because Allah (exalted is He) said, "There is nothing like Him, and He is the hearing, the seeing" (al-Shūrā 42:11) (*Al-Risāla al-qushayriyya*, 32).

Tawḥīd means believing that Allah's beautiful names and attributes are ancient and not likening Him to anything that exists or could be imagined or thought of.

Whatever a person imagines out of ignorance that He is like, the intellect indicates that He is different from it (*Al-Risāla al-qushayriyya*, 34).

The intellect confirms that anything that may be imagined about the nature of Allah is an illusion that results from ignorance.

---

[1] N/A-322 H / N/A-934 CE. He was originally from Baghdad where he accompanied Abū al-Ḥusayn al-Nūrī and al-Junayd al-Baghdādī. He later moved to Egypt and died there.

Abū Al-Ḥasan Khayr Al-Nassāj[1]

> The best tawḥīd by any creature is still incomplete because he depends on and needs someone else. Allah (exalted is He) said, "O people, you are the ones in need of Allah", so you need Him in every breath you take; and "And Allah is the one who is free of need", of you, your tawḥīd, and your actions, "the Praiseworthy" (Fāṭir 35:15) who accepts from you what He does not need and rewards you for what you need (*Ṭabaqāt al-ṣūfiyya*, 249).

A creature's tawḥīd remains imperfect because every creature depends on others. All creatures depend on Allah, who does not need anyone. One aspect of His generosity is that He rewards them for worshipping Him even though He does not need to be worshipped and it is the worshippers who need to worship Him.

---

[1] 202-322 H / 818-934 CE. He was originally from Samarra but lived in Baghdad. He accompanied Sarī al-Saqaṭī.

Abū Al-Ḥasan ʿAlī Ibn Muḥammad Al-Muzayyin[1]

Intimate knowledge is to know Allah (exalted is He) as having absolute Lordship and to know yourself in terms of servanthood. It is also to know that Allah Almighty is the first of everything, by Him exists everything, to Him belongs the fate of everything, and from Him is the sustenance of everything (*Ṭabaqāt al-ṣūfiyya*, 289).

Knowing Allah is to believe that He is the only Lord, everything is a servant of His, and the beginning, continuity, and end of everything are in His hands.

Tawḥīd is to affirm Allah's oneness through intimate knowledge, to affirm His oneness through worship, and to affirm His oneness by referring to Him in every matter, whether for you or against you. It is also to know that whatever occurs to your heart or you can allude to, Allah (exalted is He) is different from it. Furthermore, it is to know that His attributes are different from the attributes of His creatures. He differs from them in the ancientness of His attributes as they differ from Him in the origination of their attributes (*Ṭabaqāt al-ṣūfiyya*, 290).

Tawḥīd is belief and action. Belief includes exalting Allah over everything that exists or may be imagined and differentiating between His attributes and the attributes of His creatures, even when sharing the same words. His attributes are ancient whereas the attributes of His creation are originated by Him. The tawḥīd

[1] N/A-328 H / N/A-940 CE. He was from Baghdad. He accompanied Sahl al-Tustarī and al-Junayd al-Baghdādī. He lived in Mecca.

by action is to worship only Him, put one's trust in Him, and refer to His judgement in every matter.

> The belief of the people of the truth regarding His oneness is that Allah (exalted is He) is not missing to be looked for nor has an end so He may be reached. If a seeker attains something existent and known, he is deluded by the existent. For us, an extant thing is known through a spiritual state or knowledge without a spiritual state. This is so because the Real One has the attribute of oneness, which describes His being. Nothing is like Him, and He is not like things. Tawḥīd is to ascribe firstness and lastness to Him alone, excluding everything else. Our Lord is exalted over having equals and likes (*Ḥilyat al-awliyā'*, vol. 10, 341).

Allah cannot be known as things are known because He is unique, unlike anything else, and is unattainable to the sources of knowledge: the senses, the intellect, and spiritual revelation. Tawḥīd is to confess that He was before and will be after everything and that He has no likes or peers.

ʿAbd Allah Ibn Muḥammad Al-Murtaʿish Al-Naysābūrī[1]

The foundations of tawḥīd are three things: knowing Allah (exalted is He) as having Lordship, acknowledging his oneness, and denying that He has any peers (*Ṭabaqāt al-ṣūfiyya*, 267).

Tawḥīd is based on believing that Allah is the Lord of everything, is one, and has no equivalent.

[1] N/A-328 H / N/A-940 CE. He lived and died in the now extinct al-Shūnīziyya Mosque, Baghdad. He accompanied al-Junayd al-Baghdādī.

Jaʿfar Abū Bakr Al-Shiblī[1]

Whoever answers a question about tawḥīd with descriptions is a deviator. Whoever alludes to Him is a dualist. Whoever goes silent about Him is ignorant. Whoever wrongly thinks that he has become close (to Him) has not achieved anything. Whoever gestures about Him is an idol worshipper. Whoever speaks in detail about Him is oblivious. Whoever thinks he is near is remote. Whoever claims to have found Him misses Him. Everything that you discern with your imaginations and recognise with your intellects in your most perfect way is dismissed, rejected back to you, and originated and fashioned like you (*Al-Lumaʿ*, 50).

Speaking and thinking about Allah and referring to Him as with others is a delusion and falsehood. Allah is out of the reach of the intellect and imagination because they and everything they produce are originated. What is originated cannot comprehend what is ancient.

He said to a man, "Do you know why your tawḥīd is unsound?" The man replied, "No". He said, "Because you are seeking Him by yourself" (*Al-Lumaʿ*, 53).

For the servant's tawḥīd to be sound, he must make himself an instrument in Allah's hand, which means surrendering to and

[1] 247/334 H / 862/946 CE. He was born in Samarra, Iraq, but his father was from the village of Shibliyya, Khorasan. He repented in the assembly of Khayr al-Nassāj, accompanied al-Junayd al-Baghdādī, and became one of the luminaries of Sufism. He has a divan, and many sayings by him have been reported. He was a Malikī jurist. He is buried in al-Khayzarān cemetry in al-Aʿẓamiyya, Baghdad.

relying on Him. He would then see his own effort as enablement by Allah and use it to carry out His will.

> A person's tawḥīd would not be sound until his self-denial becomes His confirmation. When he was asked what he meant by "His confirmation", he replied, "Dropping all me's" (*Al-Luma'*, 54).

Sound tawḥīd is achieved only if the person denies his own power and confirms Allah's power by not attributing actions to himself, as in saying "*lī* (for me)", *bī* (by me)", and *minnī* (from me)", and any use of the possessive "*ī*".

> The person who becomes acquainted with an atom of the knowledge of tawḥīd becomes too weak to carry a mosquito because of the heaviness of his load (*Al-Luma'*, 54).

Tawḥīd is a vast science whose great intellectual and behavioural implications use up the person's capacity.

> The person who becomes acquainted with an atom of the knowledge of tawḥīd carries the heavens and the earth on his eyebrow (*Al-Luma'*, 54).

The knowledge of tawḥīd is so great that it minimises everything else in the eyes of the muwaḥḥid.

> Tawḥīd as exercised by human nature is fearing retributions and tawḥīd as focusing on divinity is one of glorification (*Al-Luma'*, 54).

When tawḥīd reflects the human nature of the muwaḥḥid, it manifests in fear of Allah's punishment. When tawḥīd reflects the Creator's divinity, it manifests in glorifying Him.

> Every allusion to the Real One by creatures is rejected back to them until they allude to the Real One by the Real One. They do not have any other way (*Al-Luma*ʿ, 295).

Describing Allah in any way other than how He described Himself in the Qur'an is a delusion.

> The tawḥīd by the person who is made one is that Allah makes you one for Him, makes you dedicated only to Him, makes you witness that, and then makes you too engrossed with Him to be aware of what He made you witness. This is tawḥīd by the elect (*Al-Luma*ʿ, 424).

The tawḥīd of the elite is Allah making the person too occupied with Him to be aware of anything else.

> How can your tawḥīd be sound when every time you possess something it possesses you and every time you see something it imprisons you? (*Ṭabaqāt al-ṣūfiyya*, 264).

Tawḥīd by the person who is possessed by this world's affairs is not sound because it requires complete servanthood, i.e., the servant being possessed by Allah alone.

> The Wāḥid is He who was known before the limits and the letters existed (*Al-Risāla al-qushayriyya*, 25).

Allah is older than all physical and nonphysical limits and His speech is older than the letters of the oldest language.

> He was asked about Allah's (exalted is He) words, "The Gracious is established on the Throne" (Ṭāhā 20:5), so he said, "The Gracious has existed from eternity, the Throne is originated, and the Throne became established by the Gracious" (*Al-Risāla al-qushayriyya*, 34).

Allah is eternal whereas the Throne is created. Being established is a state of the Throne caused by Allah.

> Oneness is an intrinsic attribute of the One whose oneness is affirmed, and it is an adornment of the muwaḥḥid (*Al-Risāla al-qushayriyya*, 494).

Allah's oneness is eternal, not a description conferred on Him by a creature. This is why the following verse mentions Allah's testimony to His oneness first and separates it from the testimonies of the angels and the people of knowledge, "Allah testifies that there is no God except Him, and so do the angels and those of knowledge, that He stands with justice. There is no God except Him, the Mighty, the Wise" (Āl ʿImrān 3:18). Tawḥīd is a noble state originating from Allah's oneness, which shows on the muwaḥḥid.

> The intimate knower does not notice anyone other than Him, does not utter words other than His, and does not see a protector of himself other than Allah (exalted is He) (*Al-Risāla al-qushayriyya*, 514).

The person who knows Allah through obedience and nearness does not see anyone else, does not speak other than what He makes him say, and does not put his trust in anyone else.

Muḥammad Ibn ʿAbd Al-Jabbār Al-Niffarī[1]

> He said to me, "If you see Me, anything other than Me that you see with your eye and heart would separate you from Me" (*Al-Mawāqif*, 25).[2]

When a servant reaches the station of seeing Allah with his heart, seeing anything else with his eyes or heart would distance him from his Lord.

> He said to me, "'And those who strive in Our cause' (al-ʿAnkabūt 29:69) [are] those who saw Me, so when I disappeared, they covered their eyes out of jealousy lest they associate someone else with Me in vision" (*Al-Mawāqif*, 25).

The *general* meaning of jihād is resisting an enemy. At times, it has the *specific* meaning of fighting an aggressor. But its *permanent* meaning is opposing one's inner enemy, the self, "the self commands evil" (Yūsuf 12:53). When a group of Muslims came back from a military expedition, the Prophet (PBUH) said to them, "You have come in the best of arrivals from the lesser jihād to the greater jihād". When he was asked about the meaning of "the greater jihād", he replied, "the servant's striving against his base desires". This is the striving that verse 29:69 refers to. Those striving for Allah's cause who reach the station of seeing Him so

---

[1] N/A-354 H / N/A-965 CE. He was from Niffar in the Qādisiyya, in modern southern Iraq. He did not write down his thoughts so it is believed that one of his students, his son, or his grandson compiled them. The quotes are from his books *al-Mawāqif* (*Sayings*) and *al-Mukhāṭabāt* (*Addresses*), which consist of spiritual revelations in the form of speech from Allah to him.

[2] The number in the source of each quote is the number of that saying or address, not its page number in the source.

they no longer see anything else cover their eyes if He becomes invisible to them to stop their vision from associating something else with Him.

> [He said to me,] "I am not in something, nor do I mix with something, nor do I dwell in something. I am not subject to 'in', nor 'from', nor 'about', nor 'how', nor 'what'. It is said, I am I, one, singular, self-sufficient, alone, alone" (*Al-Mawāqif*, 49).

He is exalted over localisation and likening. It is wrong to speak about or describe Him the way others are referred to.

> [He said,] "O servant! I have made you Mine, so if you would want other than Me to know about you you would associate with Me, and if you would hear from other than Me you would associate with Me. I am your Lord who has made you for Himself, has chosen you to speak to, and has shown you the station of everything relative to Him so that you know that you have no station in anything without Him. Your station is seeing Him, and His singling you out is being in His presence" (*Al-Mukhāṭabāt*, 2).

Allah may choose a servant for Himself, gift him with spiritual revelations, make his station seeing Him, and favour him with being in His presence. If such a servant would then occupy himself with anyone other than Him or would even make him aware of his state, he would have associated him with Allah.

> [He said,] "O servant, you are a slave of what owns you! O servant, if you see Me as it tries to own you yet it still owns you, beware that I may decree that you are a polytheist!" (*Al-Mukhāṭabāt*, 24).

The person is a servant of who possesses him. If he allows

something other than Allah to possess him after witnessing that He is the Master of everything, he would be in danger of committing polytheism.

> [He said,] "O servant! Think of two who meet, one of whom is captivated by the speech of the other while the latter is captivated by seeing the former; which one of them is more truthful in claiming love for the other? O servant! The person who is captivated by a speech commits polytheism, whereas the person who is captivated by the speaker exercises sincerity. Similarly, no matter how much I draw you near to Me with remembrance and wisdom, focus on who draws you near, not what you are drawn with" (*Al-Mukhāṭabāt*, 37).

The true muwaḥḥid seeks only the Wāḥid. He sees even his remembrance of His Lord and the wisdom that He confers on him as means that draw him near to his goal: Allah. The perfect muwaḥḥid is never occupied away from his Lord by the means or gifts that bring him closer to Him.

> [He said,] "O servant! I am the everlasting, so eternities do not inform about Me. I am the Wāḥid, so numbers are not like Me.

Allah's existence preceded everything, including time. His oneness is unique, not like numerical oneness.

> O servant! I am the Manifest so the eyes cannot see Me, and I am the Hidden so conjectures cannot reach Me" (*Al-Mukhāṭabāt*, 56).

Allah is uniquely manifest as He is invisible to the eyes, and He is uniquely hidden as thoughts and guesses cannot know me.

Anonymous[1]

Tawḥīd requires faith, so whoever is without faith has no tawḥīd. Faith requires Sharīʿa, so whoever does not observe Sharīʿa has no faith and no tawḥīd. Sharīʿa requires good manners, so whoever is without good manners has no Sharīʿa, faith, or tawḥīd (Al-Jalājilī al-Baṣrī, *Al-Lumaʿ*, 196).

Tawḥīd, having belief, following Sharīʿa, and having good manners are inseparably connected. If a person falls short on one of them, the rest would also be incomplete.

[Poverty] is the first of the stages of tawḥīd (Naṣr Ibn al-Ḥamāmī, *Al-Lumaʿ*, 75).

Sufis have made poverty their first attribute because they consider abandoning everything for the sake of Allah the first rank of tawḥīd.

The intellect has proof, wisdom has allusions, and intimate knowledge has testimonies. The intellect provides proof, wisdom gives allusions, and intimate knowledge testifies. Purity of the acts of worship cannot be achieved without purity of tawḥīd (Abū al-Ṭayyib al-Marāghī, *Al-Risāla al-qushayriyya*, 26).

The intellect confirms the oneness of Allah by logical proofs,

---

[1] I have collated in this section four sayings of four Sufis whose biographies and even years of death I could not find and another four anonymous sayings. I have put these Sufis in this position in the book because at least some of them lived before 378/989, which is when al-Ṭūsī, the author of the earliest of the two sources that mention them, died, while the others lived no later than 437/1045, which is when the other source, *al-Risāla al-Qushayriyya*, was written.

wisdom points to His oneness by realising subtle pointers in the creation, and intimate knowledge confirms Allah's oneness by the spiritual revelations and unveilings. Worshipping cannot be pure unless the servant's tawḥīd is pure.

> Intimate knowledge is a noun that means the presence of veneration in the heart that prevents you from denying Allah's names and attributes and likening Him to anything (Abū Bakr Al-Zāhir Abādhī, *Al-Risāla al-qushayriyya*, 26).

Having intimate knowledge means that the servant's glorification of Allah is such that he cannot deny the ancientness of the attributes and names that He described Himself with or liken Him to anything.

> A scholar was asked about tawḥīd, to which he replied, "It is certitude". The inquirer replied, "Explain to me what it is". The scholar said, "It is your knowledge that the motion and stillness of creatures are by the action of Allah (majestic and exalted is He) alone, without a partner. If you believe that, you affirm His oneness" (Anonymous, *Al-Risāla al-qushayriyya*, 31).

Tawḥīd is to know with certainty that the Creator is behind all the abilities and power a creature has.

> Everyone wants to allude to Him but He did not make this possible (Anonymous, *Al-Luma*ʿ, 295).

The possibility of pointing to everything makes the human being try to point to Allah also. But He is not a thing so He is beyond pointing.

> Tawḥīd is to forget everything other than tawḥīd by tawḥīd (Anonymous, *Al-Luma*ʿ, 52).

Tawḥīd becomes perfect when it pervades the intellect and senses so the person forgets everything else.

> [Higher knowledge] is the realisation of the heart by confirming His oneness in the perfection of His attributes and names. For He alone has glory, power, authority, and greatness. He is the everliving, the everlasting, the one who "there is nothing like Him, and He is the hearing, the seeing" (al-Shūrā 42:11). He is without a condition, equivalent, or likeness. This is achieved by having the hearts deny that He has opposites or peers and reject all means (Anonymous, *Al-Luma'*, 63).

Intimate knowledge means that the heart becomes aware that Allah alone has the perfection of attributes, is the supremely reigning king, is without likes, and is the Creator of all means.

Abū Ṭālib al-Makkī[1]

Allah (exalted is He) said—and His prophets were truthful[2]—to His Messenger, "So know that there is no god except Allah and ask forgiveness for your sin and for the believing men and believing women. Allah knows of your movement and your resting place" (Muḥammad 47:19). He also said, commanding His servants with the same, "know that it was revealed with the knowledge of Allah and that there is no god except Him" (Hūd 11:14). The obligation of tawḥīd is the belief of the heart that Allah (exalted is He) is one not because He is countable and He is first without a second.

Allah's oneness does not mean that He is countable because countability is an attribute of things and Allah is not a thing. Allah's firstness does not mean that He precedes something that comes after Him. Allah's oneness and firstness have unique meanings, so He is the Wāḥid without a second and the First without one that follows Him.

He is existent, no doubt; present and never absent; knowledgeable and never ignorant; able and never unable; everliving and never dies; vigilant and never oblivious; forbearing and never reckless; hearing and seeing; and a king whose kingdom never comes to an end. He is ancient

---

[1] N/A-386 H / N/A-996 CE. He was born in Iraq but migrated to Mecca. He then left for Basra and later for Baghdad. His book *Qūtu al-qulūb*, which is the source of the relatively long quote here, is one of the books that greatly influenced Abū Ḥāmid al-Ghazālī, helped him become a Sufi, and left a clear impact on his writings.

[2] The prophets truthfully conveyed what Allah revealed to them.

outside of time and He is last without a limit.

His ancientness means that He preceded time because He created it. His lastness does not mean that He is at the end of something or after it.

He has always been, and beingness is an attribute of His, not something that He originated for Himself. He is everlasting forever with no end to His everlastingness. Everlastingness is an attribute of His, not something that He originated for Himself. There is no beginning to his being, no firstness for His ancientness, and no end for His eternity. He is the last in His firstness and the first in His lastness.

He is "first" without having a "second", and He is "last" without having someone before Him.

His names, attributes, and lights are not created for Him nor are they separate from Him.

His names, attributes, and lights are ancient like Him, not originated.

He is in front of everything, behind everything, above everything, with everything, and closer to everything than itself. Despite that, He is not an abode for things and things are not an abode for Him. He is settled on the Throne as He wished, without conditioning and resemblance. He knows everything, is capable of everything, and encompasses everything…

Allah is the Creator of space and its laws, so they are under His control and do not apply to Him. He is the closest to everything without mixing with it.

> ...He (exalted is He) has names, attributes, power, greatness, speech, will, and lights all of which are not created or originated. Rather, He has always been and existed with all of His names, attributes, speech, lights, and will. His is kingship, kingdom, honour, and might. His is the creation, command, authority, and conquering. He rules with His commands in His creation and kingdom whatever He wills however He wills. There is no reviewer of His ruling. No servant has will without His will. If He wills something it happens, and nothing happens other than what He wills. No servant can avoid disobeying Him except by His mercy, and no servant can obey Him except by His love.

The names and attributes of Allah are as ancient as He is. It is only by Allah's favour that the servant avoids disobeying Him and obeys Him. The Prophet (PBUH) said, "There is none whose deeds would entitle him to get into Paradise". He was asked, "Not even you, Messenger of Allah?" He replied, "Not even I unless my Lord wraps me in Mercy".[1]

> He is alone in all of this, with no partner or helper in any of it (*Qūt al-qulūb*, 1171-1172).

Allah is one with no associates in His attributes, names, will, or actions.

---

[1] Muslim, *Al-Ṣaḥīḥ,* 2816.

Abū ʿAlī Al-Daqqāq[1]

When he became very ill late in his life, he said, "One sign of support (from Allah) is maintaining tawḥīd at the times of the passing of decrees". Referring to his poor health, he went on to explain his words, "That He has the scissors of power to carry out the decrees, cutting you piece after piece, while you remain thankful, praising" (*Al-Risāla al-qushayriyya*, 497).

Tawḥīd is the complete surrender to His will. This means not only being patient and not complaining when calamities strike but also continuing to thank and praise Him.

[1] N/A-405 H / N/A-1015 CE. He was from Neyshabur. He accompanied Abū al-Qāsim al-Naṣrābādhī. He is the Shaikh and father-in-law of Abū al-Qāsim al-Qushayrī, the author of the famous eponymous book, *al-Risāla al-qushayriyya.*

ʿAlī Al-Hajwīrī[1]

Tawḥīd is affirming the oneness of something. It is not possible to make such a ruling without knowledge. Therefore, the people of Sunna have asserted the oneness of Allah through realisation. They have seen subtle fashioning and splendid and wonderful acting. They have witnessed many subtleties and they have seen the impossibility of these manufactured things coming into existence by themselves. They have seen signs of origination visible on everything. Inevitably, there is a doer to bring them into existence from nonexistence. That is, all of the following must have a fashioner: the world, earth, heaven, sun, moon, land, seas, mountains, deserts—in their many forms, motions, and stillnesses—knowledge, speech, death, and life. They do not need two or three fashioners.

Tawḥīd is visible in the wonders of the creation and in the fact that everything is originated, having come into existence at a particular time. As things cannot create themselves, there must be a Creator. The creation also proves the oneness of the Creator because if there were more than one god, this consistency and harmony in the creation would not have existed and the creation would not have endured, "Had there been in the heavens and earth gods other than Allah, they both would have been ruined. So exalted is Allah, the Lord of the Throne, above what they describe" (al-Anbiyāʾ 21:22), "And there has never been a god with Him.

[1] N/A-465 H / N/A-1072 CE. He was born in Ghazni, Afghanistan. He met Abū al-Qāsim al-Qushayrī. His most famous work is *Kashf al-Maḥjūb*, which he wrote in Persian. The quotations in this book are from an Arabic translation.

Otherwise, each god would have taken away what it created, and some of them would have been superior to others. Exalted is Allah above what they describe" (al-Mu'minūn 23:91).

> The fashioner, the Wāḥid, the perfect, the everliving, the knowing, the aware, the capable, the chooser is in no need of a partner or other associates. As an action must have an actor and an action does not need two actors, inevitably He is one, without any doubt or uncertainty; this is certain knowledge (*Kashf al-maḥjūb*, 520-521).

This Creator must know everything, be capable of everything, and possess all attributes that make Him in no need of others. As this Creator does not need anything, there is no need for there to be another god.

Abū Ḥāmid Al-Ghazālī[1]

Tawḥīd consists of four ranks, which are the core, the core of the core, the husk, and the husk of the husk. To make this easy to understand for the unsophisticated, let's liken it to walnuts in their external husk. They have two husks and a core, and the core has oil that is the core of the core.

The first rank of tawḥīd is when a person says "there is no God except Allah" with his tongue while his heart is heedless of it or denying it, like the tawḥīd of the hypocrites.

The second is when his heart believes the meaning of the statement like the Muslim public believes it. This is the belief of laypeople.

The third is when he views it in unveilings through the lights of the truth. This is the station of those who are drawn close. He sees many things but he sees them all, despite their numerousness, coming from the Conquering Wāḥid.

The fourth is to not see existent other than One. This is

---

[1] 450-505 H / 1058-1111 CE. He was born in Khorasan. He travelled to Hejaz, Baghdad, Syria, and Egypt. He was an outstanding scholar with a wide reputation. He authored many books on the principles of Jurisprudence, theology, and others. He was a highly skilled debater and polemicist. In 484/1091, the Seljuk Vizier Niẓām al-Dīn put him in charge of the Niẓāmiyya school in Baghdad. During the four years of teaching there, he was influenced by his study of Sufism and attendance of the assemblies of Shaikh Abū ʿAlī al-Faḍl al-Fārmdhī, a student of Abū al-Qāsim al-Qushayrī. After quiting teaching at Niẓāmiyya, he left Baghdad and led a Sufi ascetic life in which he travelled to several cities, including Damasuc and Jerusalem. He went back to his birth place of Tous, where he died.

the witnessing of the truthful. Sufis call it annihilation in tawḥīd because as the person does not see other than One, he does not see himself as well. When he does not see himself because of being engrossed in tawḥīd, he does not see himself due to the annihilation of his self in his tawḥīd. This means that he does not see himself and the creation.

In the first rank, tawḥīd is only verbal; in the second, the heart confirms what is on the tongue; in the third, tawḥīd in the heart is combined with spiritual witnessing; and in the fourth, the muwaḥḥid does not see anyone other than Allah, which is the tawḥīd sought by Sufis.

The person of the first rank is a muwaḥḥid only by tongue. This protects him in this world from the sword and spearheads.

Verbal tawḥīd is not a true belief in Allah's oneness but feigning Islam because tawḥīd is the foundation of Islam, and the heart, not the tongue, is the measure of truthfulness. This hypocrisy makes people treat the hypocrite as a Muslim but he will be exposed on the Day of Resurrection.

The second is a muwaḥḥid in the sense that he believes in his heart his words, so his heart is free of denying what has become bound to it. It is a bond in the heart but with no expansion and spaciousness in it. Yet it protects the person from the torment of the hereafter if he dies in that state and actions of disobedience have not weakened its bond. There are methods that are intended to weaken and dissolve this bond, which are called "innovations". There are also methods that are intended to repel the methods of dissolving and weakening, which are also intended to strengthen this bond and tighten it in the heart. These are called *kalām* (Islamic theology), and its expert is called *mutakallim* (theologian). He is the opposite of the innovator. His intention is to repel the innovator from dissolving this bond from the hearts of laypeople. The theologian may also particularly be called a muwaḥḥid because with his theology he protects the meaning of the statement of tawḥīd in the hearts of laypeople so that its bond does not dissolve.

This is the tawḥīd of lay Muslims in which the heart confirms the declaration of the tongue. It is susceptible to the influence of innovations. Islamic theology was developed to counter them by proving the foundations of faith, the first of which is tawḥīd. Contrary to verbal tawḥīd, it saves the muwaḥḥid from the punishment on the Day of Resurrection.

The third is a muwaḥḥid in the sense that he does not see other than One Doer when the truth is disclosed to him as it is. He does not see a real doer other than One, as the truth has been disclosed to him as it is because he tasked his heart with keeping the bond of the statement of truth. That is the rank of laypeople and theologians because the theologian does not differ from the layperson in belief but in the trade of theologising with which the innovator is prevented from dissolving that bond.

Spiritual witnessing elevates the tawḥīd of the lay Muslim, theologian or not, to a rank in which the muwaḥḥid sees Allah as the only true Doer, even though he sees numerous apparent doers.

The fourth is a muwaḥḥid in the sense he does not give presence in what he witnesses to other than the Wāḥid. He does not see all things from the perspective of their numerousness but from the perspective that He is One.

This is the ultimate aim of tawḥīd.

The highest rank of tawḥīd is annihilation whereby the muwaḥḥid does not see anyone existent other than Allah, so he does not see even himself. This is the tawḥīd of the elite.

The first is like the walnut's external husk, the second is like the internal husk, the third is like the core, and the fourth is like the oil that is extracted from the core.

There is no good in the external husk of walnuts. If it is eaten, it tastes bitter. If its inside is viewed, it looks ugly. If it is used as woodfuel, it extinguishes the fire and produces much smoke. If it is left in the house, it reduces the space. Therefore, it is not good for anything other than being left to protect the walnut for a period and is then thrown away. Likewise, tawḥīd by the tongue without confirmation in the heart is useless, very harmful, and loathsome outwardly and inwardly. But it is useful for a while in protecting the internal husk until the time of death. The internal husk is the heart and the body. The tawḥīd of the hypocrite protects his body from the sword of the conquerers for they have not been commanded to open up hearts, and the sword only affects the body, which is the husk. The body leaves the person when he dies, so his tawḥīd becomes useless after that.

Tawḥīd by tongue only is not real. It protects the person from the accusation of disbelief in this world, but it does not save him from the fire in the hereafter.

As the internal husk has clear benefits over the external husk, it also protects the core and guards it against rotting when stored. When removed, it can be benefited from as woodfuel. But it has a lower status than the core.

Tawḥīd by tongue and heart protects the person from the Fire but it has the lowest status among the ranks of true tawḥīd.

> Similarly, the mere belief without unveilings is much more beneficial than the mere uttering of the tongue, but it is lacking in status relative to the unveiling and witnessing that happen by the expansion and spaciousness of the heart and shining of the light of truth in it. That is the expansion meant by the Almighty's words, "So whoever Allah wants to guide, He expands his breast for Islam" (al-Anʿām 6:125), and, "Is he whose breast Allah has expanded for Islam so he has a light from his Lord?" (al-Zumar 39:22).

Spiritual unveilings elevate what may be described as tawḥīd by the heart, which combines rational conviction and emotional surrender, to what may be described as tawḥīd by witness. The latter is based on, in addition to the conviction of the mind and comfort of the heart, spiritual supernatural experiences, such as sleep visions and wakefulness revelations.

> While the core is intrinsically valuable in comparison with the husk and it is the intended target, it is not free of extraction residues, unlike the oil that is extracted from it. Similarly, actual tawḥīd is a sublime goal for the seekers but it is not free from the impurities of paying attention to others and being distracted by numerousness in comparison with the person who does not see other than the Real Wāḥid (*Iḥyāʾ ʿulūm al-dīn*, 1604-1605).

The highest rank of tawḥīd is that of the person who attains annihilation so that he does not see other than Allah.

Arslān Al-Dimashqī[1]

You are all full of hidden polytheism. You will not have tawḥīd until you have departed yourself and everything other than Him. The more sincere you are, the more He reveals to you that it is He, not you, so you ask Him for forgiveness for being yourself.

Conspicuous polytheism is claiming that there is a god other than Allah, but being occupied with any creature, even one's self, is also polytheism, albeit hidden. The more the servant's sincerity to his Lord, the greater his awareness by the intellect and the heart that Allah is the true doer of everything. He would then seek forgiveness for even having a will other than Allah's will, "I have not created the jinn and mankind except to worship Me" (al-Dhāriyāt 51:56).

Whenever you affirm His oneness, polytheism becomes clear to you, so you renew your tawḥīd and your faith every hour all the time. The more you depart all others, the more your faith increases. The more you depart yourself, the stronger your certitude becomes.

Affirming Allah's oneness exposes the various forms of polytheism. The more the person forsakes creatures, the stronger his faith becomes, and the more he abandons himself, the more certain he becomes.

O prisoner of pleasures and worship, O prisoner of

---

[1] 470-541 H / 1077-1146 CE. He was born in the village of Ja'bar, Syria. He learned at the hands of Shaikh Abū 'Āmir al-Mu'addib. It looks like he had books and epistles that did not survive with the exception of his epistle on tawḥīd. He is also reported to have composed poetry.

> stations and unveilings! You are conceited. You are occupied with yourself away from Him. Where is being occupied with Him away from you? He (majestic and exalted is He) is present and seeing, "He is with you wherever you are" (al-Ḥadīd 57:4), in this world and the hereafter. If you are with Him, He veils you from yourself. If you are with yourself, He takes you as a servant.

Even seeking spiritual stations and unveilings is a form of occupation with other than Allah because it represents seeking something other than Him. These are desires of the self. The Lord observes the servant all the time, whereas the servant does not see his Lord as long as he is occupied with himself. The self is a barrier to nearness to Allah and a veil to seeing Him. The person who sees himself has to actively seek to worship, but when he forgets himself and achieves annihilation, he attains servanthood. Perfect servanthood is not realised until the servant becomes occupied with the Worshipped One only and forgets everything else, including himself. Then he comes to be with Allah without veils, becomes in permanent worship, and servanthood becomes his natural and permanent state.

> Faith is departing them and certitude is departing yourself. When your faith increases, you are transferred from one state to another. When your certitude increases, you are transferred from one station to another (*Risāla fī al-tawḥīd*, 107-108).

Faith is to abandon all creatures and see the Creator only. Certitude is higher than faith because it involves abandoning the self also in seeking the Creator. The increase in faith raises the believer from one spiritual state to a higher one, whereas the increase in certitude lifts the certain person from one spiritual station to a more sublime one.

> The believer sees with Allah's light and the intimate knower sees Him by Him. As long as you are with yourself, We command you. When you are annihilated, We take command of you. He would not take command of them until they are annihilated. As long as you are, you are a seeker. When He annihilates your self, you become sought after. The longer-lasting certitude is in being absent to yourself and present by Him. How great the difference is between being by His command and being by Him!

Faith is light from Allah that makes the believer see the world and what happens in it, including what occurs to him, as being done and enabled by Allah. The intimate knower, on the other hand, is annihilated for Allah's sake so he himself has become a means in the hand of Allah, showing him with His light what He wants. Faith is a state of consciousness of Allah whereas intimate knowledge is a state of complete surrender to Allah so that the consciousness of the servant becomes in Allah's hand. When the self is present and has an influence, the believer actively works to obey Allah. When he becomes annihilated, his obedience to Allah becomes natural. The state of certitude is one in which the self of the servant is annihilated so that he exists only for Allah. The person who fully surrenders so that all his affairs rest in Allah's hand, becoming a tool that Allah moves as He wishes, is in a far more noble state than the person who manages his affairs as Allah wants.

> If you exist by His command, the means submit to you; if you exist by Him, the worlds are humbled for you (*Risāla fī al-tawḥīd*, 108-109).

Complete faith puts means at the service of the servant, giving him authority over things. Annihilation puts the multiverse at the service of the servant. In one Qudsī ḥadīth,[1] the Prophet (PBUH) reported this speech of Allah, "My servant continues to draw near to Me by performing supererogatory acts of worship until I love him. When I love him, I become his hearing with which he hears, his sight with which he sees, his hand with which he strikes, and his leg with which he walks. If he asks Me for something, I surely give it to him, and if he seeks refuge in Me, I surely protect him".[2]

---

[1] A Qudsī ḥadīth is a non-verbal revelation from Allah that the Prophet Muḥammad (PBUH) expressed in his own words.

[2] Al-Bukhārī, *Al-Ṣaḥīḥ,* 6273.

ʿAbd Al-Qādir Al-Jīlānī[1]

[2]Give up what is in the hands of creatures, so do not seek it and do not make your heart attached to it. Do not have hope in creatures or fear them. Take from the favour of Allah (majestic and exalted is He), which is "what does not cause you doubt". Have one Chief, one Giver, One that you have hope from, One you fear, and One source of power, which is your Lord (majestic and exalted is He). It is He in whose hand are the forelocks[3] of kings. The hearts of creatures, which are the commanders of the bodies, are in His hand. The property of the creatures is all His (majestic and exalted is He). Creatures are His agents and trustees, so their hand movements when they give you anything are by His permission (majestic and exalted is He), and the same applies to the refraining of their hands from giving you. Allah (majestic and exalted is He) said, "And ask Allah of His bounty" (al-Nisāʾ 4:32), and He (majestic and exalted is He) said, "Those whom you worship other than Allah do not have provision for you.

---

[1] 470-561 H / 1077-1165 CE. He was born in Gaylān, north of today's Iran. When he was eighteen, he migrated to Baghdad where he spent many years travelling, worshipping in seclusion, and seeking knowledge. He later accompanied Abū Saʿīd al-Makhzūmī, who gave him his school, where he taught for forty years until his death and was buried there. The quotations in this book are from his sermons at the school. He has several works. The Shaikh has occupied a special place in the hearts of countless Muslims over the centuries. His great role in serving and spreading Islam shows in the fact that the Sufi orders that trace their chains of Shaikhs to him are the largest in number and size.

[2] This passage is from a commentary on this ḥadīth, "Leave what causes you doubt and turn to what does not cause you doubt" (Al-Nasāʾī, *Al-Sunan,* 5711.)

[3] The forelock is a symbol of honour and dignity.

> So seek provision from Allah, worship Him, and be grateful to Him" (al-ʿAnkabūt 29:17) (*Futūḥ al-ghayb*, 20).[1]

A common theme in Shaikh ʿAbd al-Qādir's sermons is the necessity of seeing Allah Almighty as the true doer of everything and that all creatures are instruments in His hand. This is the essence of tawḥīd. It means being indifferent to creatures and what they have and focusing wholly on Allah.

> Have you not heard these words of the Messenger (PBUH), "When Allah loves a servant, He afflicts him. If he shows patience, He acquires him". It was said, "O Messenger of Allah, what does 'acquires him' mean?" He replied, "He would not leave property or children for him".[2] The reason is that if he had property and children, he would love them, so his love for his Lord (majestic and exalted is He) would be split. It would reduce and become divided, becoming shared between Allah and others, yet Allah (exalted is He) does not accept partnership. He is jealous, conquering everything, and victorious over everything. So, He would destroy His partner and leave him with nothing to make the heart of His servant loyal to Him, without a partner. Then, these words of His (majestic and exalted is He) are fulfilled, "He loves them and they love Him" (al-Māʾida 5:54) (*Futūḥ al-ghayb*, 32).

Allah's affliction of a servant by depriving him of what he loves is a sign that He loves him and has chosen him to be a perfect muwaḥḥid. Allah becomes his only beloved and concern.

---

[1] The number in the source of each quote is that of the assembly, not its page number in the source.

[2] Ibn Abū ʿĀṣim, *Al-Āḥād wa al-mathānī*, 2499.

> Always observe His commandment, refrain from His prohibitions, surrender to His decree, and do not associate Him with any of His creations. Your will, desire, and passions are His creation, so you should have no will, desire, or passion to avoid being a polytheist. Allah (majestic and exalted is He) said, "So whoever hopes for the meeting with his Lord, let him do good work and not associate anyone in the worship of his Lord" (al-Kahf 18:110).
>
> Polytheism is not only worshipping idols, but it is also following your desires and choosing besides your Lord (majestic and exalted is He) other than Him from this world and the hereafter. Anything other than Him (majestic and exalted is He) is something else, so if you resort to other than Him, you associate with Him (majestic and exalted is He) (*Futūḥ al-ghayb*, 7).

Worshipping anyone other than Allah is conspicuous polytheism and having a will other than what Allah wants is hidden polytheism. Perfect tawḥīd is the annihilation and complete surrender to Allah.

> You have been blocked from Allah's benefits and seeking His favours first by your reliance on creatures, means, trades, and work. Creatures are your veil from earning a livelihood according to the Sunna, which is the legitimate way of earning a living. As long as you are being with creatures, hoping for their givings and favours, asking them, repeatedly knocking on their doors, you associate with Allah His creatures. He would punish you by preventing you from earning a living according to the Sunna, which is getting a livelihood from the permissible

things of this world.

Allah permitted work as a means to earn a living, so work is not an act of associating others with Him. But replacing work with seeking help from creatures amounts to abandoning what Allah permitted for what He did not make a legal means, hence it is like associating His creation with Him.

> If you then renounce depending on creatures and associating them with your Lord, resort to earning your livelihood through legitimate work, put your trust in legitimate work, feel comfortable with it, and forget the favours of the Lord (majestic and exalted is He), you would still be a polytheist. This, however, is hidden polytheism; more hidden than the first. Allah (majestic and exalted is He) would punish you by blocking you from His favours and seeking Him first (*Futūḥ al-ghayb*, 16).

Making a livelihood according to Sharīʿa without combining it with having trust in Allah and the complete belief that He is the source of every favour is also polytheism, albeit more subtle than relying on creatures instead of working.

> I saw in a dream as if I said, "O you who have associated with his Lord (majestic and exalted is He) himself in his inward, His creatures in his outward, and his will in his knowledge!" A man next to me asked, "What is this speech?" I replied, "A form of intimate knowledge" (*Futūḥ al-ghayb*, 63).

Following one's desires is hidden polytheism, relying on creatures and means is manifest polytheism, and thinking that one's will can override Allah's predestination is polytheism caused by ignorance. Godly visions are part of the spiritual life of the human being, as the Messenger (PBUH) said, "The vision of a believer is one of the forty-six parts of prophecy".[1]

> The foundation of good deeds is tawḥīd and sincerity. The person who lacks tawḥīd and sincerity has no good deeds. Perfect the foundation of your deeds by tawḥīd and sincerity then do your deeds by Allah's ability and power, not by your ability and power. The hand of tawḥīd, not the hand of polytheism and hypocrisy, is the builder. The muwaḥḥid is the one whose deeds rise, whereas the hypocrite's deeds don't (*Al-Fatḥ al-rabbānī*, 6).

Actions cannot be good deeds unless they are built on tawḥīd and sincerity to Allah. An essential requirement of good deeds is the belief that they are enabled by Allah.

> O young man! Well-being lies in abandoning the quest for well-being, affluence in giving up seeking affluence, and remedy in relinquishing the quest for remedy. All remedy is in submitting to the Real One (majestic and exalted is He) and cutting off the means and casting away the lords for your heart. The remedy lies in the tawḥīd of Allah (majestic and exalted is He) by heart, not only by tongue. Tawḥīd and renunciation do not show on the body and tongue. Tawḥīd is in the heart, renunciation is in the heart, piety is in the heart, intimate knowledge is in the heart, knowledge of the Real One is in the heart, love of Allah (majestic and exalted is He) is in the heart, and nearness to Him is in the heart (*Al-Fatḥ al-rabbānī*, 13).

Tawḥīd means total reliance on Allah, the Lord of all means. Tawḥīd and all forms of worship, even those that are physical, are in essence deeds of the heart. The Messenger said, "There is a piece

---

[1] Muslim, *Al-Ṣaḥīḥ*, 2263.

of flesh in the body if it becomes good, the whole body becomes good, but if it becomes corrupted, the whole body becomes corrupted, and that is the heart".[1]

> The Prophet (PBUH) is reported to have said, "Exhaust your devils by saying 'there is no God except Allah, Muḥammad is the Messenger of Allah' for Satan is exhausted by it as one of you exhausts his camel by riding it a lot and making it carry his loads".[2] O people! Exhaust your devils by being sincere in saying "there is no God except Allah", not only by uttering it. Tawḥīd burns the human and jinn devils because it is fire for the devils and light for the muwaḥḥids.

The sincere repetition of the testimony of tawḥīd grants the muwaḥḥid victory over the devils. Tawḥīd by the heart means trusting the Lord of means.

> How can you say "there is no God except Allah" when there are many lords in your heart? Everything that you depend on and trust to the exclusion of Allah (majestic and exalted is He) is an idol of yours. Tawḥīd by your tongue would not benefit you when there is polytheism in the heart. The purity of the body would not benefit you when there is impurity in the heart. The muwaḥḥid exhausts his devil, whereas the polytheist is exhausted by his devil. Sincerity is the kernel of words and deeds because when they lack it, they are a shell without a kernel. The shell is good for nothing other than fire (*Al-Fatḥ al-rabbānī*, 38).

---

[1] Al-Bukhārī, *Al-Ṣaḥīḥ*, 52.

[2] There is the following similar ḥadīth, "The believer exhausts his devils as one of you exhausts his camel during travel" (Aḥmad Ibn Ḥanbal, *Musnad*, 8940.)

Tawḥīd is a deed of the heart, so it cannot be real unless it is founded on sincerity. Worshipping by the body without the heart is a rewardless effort, as the Prophet (PBUH) said, "There may be a fasting person who earns only hunger from his fast, and there may be a person who prays at night who earns only sleeplessness from his praying".[1]

> The first stage of this matter is testifying that "there is no God except Allah, Muḥammad is the Messenger of Allah", and its last stage is seeing precious stone and clay as equal. The person whose heart is sound and connected to his Lord sees as equal praise and dispraise, sickness and good health, affluence and poverty, and good and bad fortune in this world. When this has become true of someone, his lower self and passion die, the aggression of his natural inclinations dies out, and his devil is subjugated to him (*Al-Fatḥ al-rabbānī*, 60).

The testimony of tawḥīd is only the start of one's spiritual journey. The person who becomes near to his Lord finds precious and cheap things of this world as equal, is not concerned about whether people approve or disapprove of him, and does not feel happy by gains or saddened by losses of worldly things. The muwaḥḥid who arrived at stations of nearness to Allah is annihilated in his Lord, having no will. Satan does not have any control over him because Satan's instrument, the lower self, has died because of worship and spiritual exercises.

> This way is all about annihilation and obliteration. In the beginning, when faith is still weak [the person says], "There is no God except Allah", and at the end, when faith has become strong [the person says], "There is no God

[1] Ibn Māja, *Al-Sunan,* 1690.

except You" because he addresses One who is present and witnessed (*Al-Fatḥ al-rabbānī*, 62).

Saying "there is no God except Allah" means embracing Islam and the beginning of belief. It is a testimony of those who are close to Him and those who are remote from Him. When faith has grown strong, the believer remembers Allah by tongue and heart. His tawḥīd becomes that of witnessing in which he addresses His Lord in the second person, "You". The extinction of the lower self strengthens faith and brings the person close to Allah. He becomes permanently conscious of His presence, everywhere, all the time, thus experiencing the reality of "He is with you wherever you are" (al-Ḥadīd 57:4).

Aḥmad Al-Rifāʿī[1]

[Intimate knowledge] is like a tree that has three branches: *tawḥīd*, *tajrīd*, and *tafrīd*. *Tawḥīd* means acknowledgement [of Allah's oneness], *tajrīd* means sincerity [to Him], and *tafrīd* means total dedication to Him alone in every situation.

The first step of intimate knowledge is *tawḥīd*, which is to deny any equivalents for Him; then *tajrīd*, which is abandoning all means; and *tafrīd*, which means connecting without walking, seeing, or separation. It has five routes. First, having fear privately and publicly; second, obeying Him in servanthood; third, having a total dedication to Him alone; fourth, being sincere to Him in word, deed, and intention; and fifth, being observant in every thought and look (*Ḥāl ahl al-ḥaqīqa*, 10-11).

Intimate knowledge begins with affirming His oneness, relying on Him, rather than on the means, and seeking His company only and not that of creatures. The route to intimate knowledge consists of five states that the servant must acquire. Being observant means that the servant monitors his thoughts, actions, states, and everything that he experiences to purify his inward.

"The statement 'there is no God except Allah' is My fortress. Anyone who says it enters My fortress, and

---

[1] 512-578 H / 1119-1183 CE. He was born in Wāsiṭ, Iraq. When he was twenty-eight, his Shaikh instructed him to move to the village of Ūmm ʿUbayda, Maysān, where he lived until his death and was buried there. He studied under ʿAlī Abū al-Faḍl and other Shaikhs. Ṭarīqa Rifāʿiyya is named after him.

anyone who enters My fortress becomes safe from My torture".[1] This Qudsī ḥadīth, which we have received through transmission from the Prophet (PBUH), reveres the statement of tawḥīd. This reverence increases the servant's faith, fills him with intimate knowledge, and obligates him to persist in repeating this declaration, which is the essence of tawḥīd. Anyone who utters it after believing in who conveyed it (PBUH) will not suffer ill fortune (*Ḥāl ahl al-ḥaqīqa*, 127).

Saying "there is no God except Allah" by both tongue and heart increases the servant's faith and brings him closer to Allah. Combining it with the belief that "Muḥammad is the Messenger of Allah" grants the servant safety.

All your tawḥīd before exalting Him is polytheism. Tawḥīd is ecstasy in the heart that stops denying Allah's names and attributes and likening Him to anything (*Ḥikam al-Rifāʿī*, 8).

There can be no tawḥīd without exalting Allah over everything. Tawḥīd is an overwhelming love in the heart that stops the lover from denying Allah's names and attributes or likening Him to anything.

The Sufi stays away from illusions and doubts and affirms the oneness of Allah (exalted is He) in being, attributes, and actions because "there is nothing like Him" (al-Shūrā 42:11). He knows that with certain knowledge, thus he exited the realm of conjectural knowledge (*Ḥikam al-Rifāʿī*, 18).

---

[1] Al-Daylamī, *Al-Firdaws,* 8101.

The Sufi is certain that Allah has no like in essence, attributes, or actions.

Muḥyī Al-Dīn Ibn ʿArabī[1]

Allah (exalted is He) is one god without a second. He is exalted over having a female companion or a child. He is an owner without a partner, a king without a vizier, a maker without a manager with Him. He exists by Himself without the need for something to grant Him existence; rather, every existing thing needs Him to exist. The whole world exists by Him, whereas He alone exists by Himself. There is no beginning for His existence and no end for His perpetuity. His existence is absolute, unconstrained, and self-sustained.

Allah does not depend in His existence on anything for He exists by Himself. The creation, on the other hand, is originated by Him, and He is the cause of its continued existence. So Allah exists by Himself whereas everything exists by His command. He is of necessary existence and everything else is of possible existence.

He is not a localised essence to be in a particular place nor is He accidental for perpetuity to be impossible for Him. He is not corporal to have sides and a direction to Him. He is exalted over having sides and dimensions…

---

[1] 560-638 H / 1165-1240 CE. He was born in Murcia, southeastern al-Andalus. He travelled a lot in the east, visiting Mecca, Mosul, Cairo, and Konya. He lived his last fifteen years in Damascus, where he died and was buried at the foot of Mount Qasioun. Like al-Ḥallāj, Ibn ʿArabī is among the Sufis most criticised and accused of disbelief. His are among the most misunderstood Sufi words, having been accused of believing that the Creator is in the creation and the unity of the Creator and the creation. As explained in the *Introduction*, this misunderstanding is partly due to his symbolic language and its dealing with unfamiliar spiritual subjects and states, taking some of his words out of context, and ignoring his many other statements that contravene those misinterpretations.

Allah is not an essence to have to exist in something or an originated thing to disappear. He is not a body to have sides and dimensions.

> ...He does not have a comprehensible likeness nor can intellects point to Him. Time does not limit Him and space does not contain Him. He existed when there was no space, and He is now as He has always been. He created everything that is localised and space and devised time. He said, "I am the Wāḥid, the Everliving".

The intellect cannot even imagine Allah. He is the creator of time and space so He is not subject to or describable by them.

> Preserving the creatures does not tire Him. He does not acquire an attribute He did not have that belongs to made things. He is exalted over originated things to be in Him or for Him to be in them, or for them to be after Him or for Him to be before them. Rather, it is said, "He was and there was nothing with Him" because beforeness and afterness are aspects of time, which He fashioned. He is the vigilant One who never sleeps and the Conquerer who cannot be attained. "There is nothing like Him" (al-Shūrā' 42:11) (*Al-Futūḥāt al-makkiya*, vol. 1, 62).

Allah does not change, so His attributes do not change and He does not acquire attributes of creatures. Originated things do not affect Him and He does not mix with them because the created cannot be in the ancient Creator and the ancient Creator cannot be in His originated creation. The appearance and disappearance of creatures are not dated relative to His existence because time is a created thing so it applies to creatures and does not apply to the Creator.

> Tawḥīd is knowledge, then a state, then knowledge. The first knowledge is tawḥīd by proof, which is the tawḥīd of laypeople. I mean by laypeople those who have outward knowledge. Tawḥīd as a state is when the Real One becomes your attribute, so it is He, not you, in you, "And you did not throw when you threw but it was Allah who threw" (al-Anfāl 8:17). The second knowledge, which is after the state, is the tawḥīd of witnessing (*Al-Tajalliyāt al-ilāhiyya*, 18).

In its first stage, tawḥīd is rational knowledge that points to the oneness of the Creator. In the second stage, it becomes a state in which the muwaḥḥid becomes an instrument in the hand of Allah that has no will of its own. In the third stage, tawḥīd becomes knowledge in which rational knowledge and the state of annihilation are combined with unveilings and spiritual experiences that transcend mind and matter; this is the tawḥīd of spiritual witnessing.

> Allah, glorified be His praise, said in His impregnable Book, "Allah witnesses that there is no God except Him, and so do the angels and those of knowledge—[that He is] upholding justice. There is no God except Him, the Impregnable, the Wise" (Āl 'Imrān 3:18). Then He said, "Indeed, the religion in the sight of Allah is Islam" (Āl 'Imrān 3:19). The Messenger of Allah (PBUH) said, "Embracing Islam is to testify that there is no God except Allah and that Muḥammad is the Messenger of Allah", as in the ḥadīth.[1]
>
> The Almighty said, "and those of knowledge", and did not say, "and those of faith". His testimony in affirming

[1] Muslim, *Al-Ṣaḥīḥ*, 8.

His oneness is not derived from transmitted information for it to be faith. Likewise, a witness testimony can only be based on knowledge; otherwise, it would not be admissible.

Allah (majestic and exalted is He) then added the angels and those of knowledge using the conjunction "and". The latter indicates sharing, but this sharing is absolutely confined to the testimony. Then He related them to knowledge, not faith. We, therefore, knew that He meant those who attained tawḥīd through theoretical or necessary knowledge, not through transmitted information. It is as if He said, "The angels testified to My oneness by the necessary knowledge from revelation, which provided them with knowledge and represented sound consideration of proofs. So they testified to My oneness as I testified to Myself, and so did those of knowledge by the rational consideration that I endowed My servants with".

Tawḥīd based on knowledge is greater than when it is based on faith. The first to testify to the oneness of Allah was Allah Himself, who knows everything. The angels then testified to His oneness, the knowledge of which they acquired by unveilings. Those of knowledge testified to the oneness of Allah by the faculty of the intellect.

He mentioned faith second in ranking after knowledge, which is what prosperity depends on. Allah commanded it, and we called it "knowledge" because the source of information is Allah. He said, "So know that there is no God except Allah" (Muḥammad 47:19), and He (exalted is He) said, "And that they may know that He is one God"

> (Ibrāhīm 14:52) when He set the ranks at the end of the chapter of Ibrāhīm of the Impregnable Qur'an (*Al-Futūḥāt al-makkiya*, vol. 1, 491).

Faith is the acceptance of information about the unseen, that is, something that the person has not witnessed or concluded. The Qur'an calls the truth that Allah is the only God "knowledge" because Allah is its source. This is why Allah described faith as knowledge. Knowledge precedes faith and is its foundation because faith is the acceptance of knowledge. Therefore, knowledge is mentioned first in verse 3:18, and Islam, which is the first stage of faith, is mentioned second in verse 19. The end of the chapter of Ibrāhīm refers to the Day of Resurrection, mentions that Allah requites every soul according to its deeds, and concludes with this verse, "This is notification for the people that they may be warned thereby and that they may know that He is but one God and that those of understanding may be reminded with" (Ibrāhīm 14:52).

> Tawḥīd is an action by the muwaḥḥid with which the person knows that Allah is one. He (exalted is He) said, "Had there been gods besides Allah in the heavens and earth, they would have been ruined" (al-Anbiyā' 21:22). The existing intactness, which is the continued existence of the world, indicates that had He who made it not be one, this world would not have existed. This is the Real One's proof of His oneness in the world, which matches the rational proof (*Al-Futūḥāt al-makkiya*, vol. 3, 434).

The existence of the universe is proof that there is no god save Allah. This Qur'anic proof confirms the rational proof of His oneness.

> You have to discharge the foremost obligation towards

> Allah, which is to not associate with Allah any hidden polytheism. The latter means relying on set means, resorting to them by heart, and feeling reassured by them, which is when the heart feels at rest with them and by them. This is one of the gravest religious calamities for a believer, to which He (exalted is He) has alluded in these words, "And most of them do not believe in Allah except while they associate others with Him" (Yūsuf 12:106). This means—but Allah knows best—hidden polytheism, which involves believing in the existence of Allah while annulling the belief in tawḥīd in action, not annulling the belief in His divinity. The latter is conspicuous polytheism, which contradicts the belief in the oneness of Allah concerning divinity, not the belief in Allah's existence.

Claiming that there is a god other than Allah is conspicuous polytheism. Believing in Allah's oneness yet relying on means, instead of relying on the Lord of means, is hidden polytheism.

> It has been reported in an authentic ḥadīth of the Messenger of Allah (PBUH) that he said, "Do you know what Allah's right on His servants is?" Allah's right on His servants is that they worship Him and do not associate anything with Him".[1] He said "thing", which is indefinite, so it covers both the conspicuous and hidden forms of polytheism. He then said, "Do you know what their right on Allah is if they do that? That He would not torment them".

The word "thing" in the noble ḥadīth does not include alleged gods only, but anything other than Allah, including means.

[1] Al-Tirmidhī, *Al-Jāmiʿ al-kabīr*, 2643.

> Note his words "that He would not torment them". If they do not associate with Allah anything, nothing would occupy their minds other than Allah, for they would not turn to anything other than Allah. If they commit the association with Allah that contravenes Islam or hidden polytheism, which is to look at familiar means, then Allah has tormented them by this reliance on means because they are subject to be lost. When means are available, they are tormented by wrongly thinking that they are unavailable and by any partial loss of them. When they truly lose them, they are tormented by the loss. So they are tormented in both cases, when means are available and when they are not. But if they do not associate with Allah any means, they would be at rest and would not worry whether they are available or not. For the One on whom they rely, Allah, can make things happen in a way that they could not even imagine, as He (exalted is He) said, "And whoever fears Allah, He will make for him a way out and will provide for him from where he does not expect" (al-Ṭalāq 65:2-3) (*Al-Waṣāyā*, 51-52).

The person who is in a state of subtle polytheism is in continuous torment. When the means are available, he is in fear of losing them, and when they are unavailable, he suffers because of their unavailability. The person who does not care about the means and looks only to their Lord is in the comfort and safety of perfect tawḥīd, which is avoiding both conspicuous and hidden polytheism. This is the realisation of "there is no god save Allah".

ʿAlī Abū Al-Ḥasan Al-Shādhilī[1]

Know that in every moment, Allah has a share of servanthood in you which the Real One (glory be to Him) demands of you by authority of Lordship (*Al-Tanwīr*, 39).

One of the rights of the Lordship of Allah over the servant is that his behaviour must always manifest something that acknowledges his servanthood to Allah.

Last night was nothing but a great night. It was the Night of Decree. I saw the Messenger (PBUH) say, "O ʿAlī! Purify your clothes from impurity so that you receive support from Allah with every breath". I said, "O Messenger of Allah! What are my clothes?" He said, "Know that Allah has clothed you with five robes: the robe of love, the robe of intimate knowledge, the robe of tawḥīd, the robe of faith, and the robe of Islam. Whoever loves Allah finds everything negligible, whoever knows Allah (exalted is He) finds everything small, whoever affirms the Oneness of Allah does not associate with Him anything, whoever believes in Allah is safe from everything, and whoever surrenders to Allah does not disobey Him; but if he disobeys Him, he apologises to

[1] 593-656 H / 1197-1258 CE. He was born in Ghumara, north of Morocco. He travelled to Tunis on his way for pilgrimage and then visited Baghdad before returning to Ghumara, where he studied at the hands of ʿAbd al-Salām Ibn Mashīsh. His Shaikh instructed him to go and live in the village of "Shādhila" in Tunis, where his title came from. He told him that he would later go to Tunisia and then move east. He settled in Alexandria, Egypt. While on his way for pilgrimage, he died in Ḥumaytharā, in the desert of ʿĪdhāb, Egypt, and was buried there. The Shādhilī Ṭarīqa is one of the largest Sufi Ṭarīqas, with numerous followers in northern Africa in particular.

> Him; and when he apologises to Him, He accepts his apology". At this point I understood His (glory be to Him) words, "And your clothes, purify" (al-Muddaththir 74:4) (*Laṭā'if al-minan*, 78-79).

The profound spiritual meaning of clothes purification in verse 74:4 is that the person must have five attributes: love Allah, know Him, affirm His oneness, believe in Him, and surrender to Him.

> The Sufi is one who, deep inside, sees creatures as tiny particles in the air. They are neither existent nor inexistent, just as they are in the knowledge of the Lord of the worlds (*Laṭā'if al-minan*, 160).

The Sufi sees creatures like dust particles in the air that are so tiny that they are almost nonexistent. They exist because they have been created, and they are inexistent because their existence is not necessary but possible as their existence and continuity are caused by Allah.

> We do not see anyone of the creatures. Is there in existence anything other than the Real Sovereign? Even if there are, they would be like tiny particles in the air that you would find to be nothing when you examine them (*Laṭā'if al-minan*, 160).

The perfect muwaḥḥid sees almost no one and nothing in existence other than Allah, the Wāḥid, who is of necessary existence.

Abū Al-ʿAbbās Al-Mursī[1]

He spoke about reconciling the meanings of these two verses, "O you who have believed! Be pious towards Allah the piety He deserves and do not die except as Muslims" (Āl ʿImrān 3:102), which talks about having as much piety as Allah deserves, and "Be pious towards Allah as much as you can" (al-Taghābun 64:16), which talks about having as much piety as one can. He said "'Be pious towards Allah as much as you can' concerning actions; His words 'Be pious towards Allah the piety He deserves' concern tawḥīd. His words 'do not die except as Muslims' mean that you must perform only those actions that, should you die while doing them, you would die as Muslims" (*Laṭāʾif al-minan*, 133-134).

Muslims differ in the amount of piety in their actions. The piety manifested in the actions of one Muslim may be more or less than the piety in the actions of another. Tawḥīd, on the other hand, is an aspect of piety that must not be deficient, meaning it must be in tongue and heart, in word and deed. Therefore, Allah has commanded that it must be complete, which is the meaning of "the piety He deserves". Allah also commanded the believer to always act in accordance with Islam, so that should death arrive, he would

---

[1] 616-686 H / 1220-1287 CE. He was born in Murcia, southeastern al-Andalus, hence his title. In 640/1242, he met Abū al-Ḥasan al-Shādhilī in Tunisia and became one of his followers. Two years later, he went with his Shaikh to Alexandria, Egypt. Four years later, al-Shādhilī named Abū al-ʿAbbās as his successor. Abū al-ʿAbbās went to Cairo for preaching and would regularly visit his Shaikh in Alexandria. He accompanied his Shaikh on his trip for pilgrimage during which al-Shādhilī died so he was one of those who buried him. Abū al-ʿAbbās settled in Alexandria where he also died and was buried.

die as a practising Muslim. This is the interpretation of Joseph's prayer, "make me die as a Muslim" (Yūsuf 12:101), not him asking for death as most exegetes have said, as I explained in my detailed study of the chapter of Yūsuf.[1]

[1] Fatoohi, *The Prophet Joseph*, 186.

Ibn ʿAṭāʾ Allah Al-Sakandarī[1]

The universe is all darkness but the manifestation of the Real One in it illuminates it. Whoever sees the universe but does not witness Him in it, at it, before it, or after it has missed the existing lights and is veiled from the suns of intimate knowledge by the clouds of effects (*Al-Ḥikam al-ʿaṭāʾiyya*, 14).[2]

Nothing would have existed and been perceived without the Creator. Anyone who sees a created thing without seeing it as having been made by Allah is blinded by the sight of a created thing from realising that it must have a Maker.

How can it be conceived that something could veil Him when it is He who manifests everything?
How can it be conceived that something could veil Him when He is manifest through everything?
How can it be conceived that something could veil Him when He is manifest in everything?
How can it be conceived that something could veil Him when He is manifest to everything?
How can it be conceived that something could veil Him

---

[1] 658-709 H / 1260-1310 CE. He was born in Alexandria. He was critical of Abū Al-ʿAbbās Al-Mursī without knowing him until he accompanied him in 674 H, listening to his words, seeing his actions, and witnessing his states. He became his most prominent follower and his successor. He later moved to live in Cairo, where he died and was buried. He authored several books in which he quoted sayings of Abū al-Ḥasan al-Shādhilī and Abū al-ʿAbbās al-Mursī, both of whom did not leave any writings, thus preserving traditions of the first two Shaikhs of the Shādhilī Ṭarīqa.

[2] The number in the source of each quote is that of the saying, not its page number in the source.

when He was manifest before the existence of anything?

How can it be conceived that something could veil Him when He is more manifest than anything?

How can it be conceived that something could veil Him when He is the Wāḥid with whom there is nothing?

How can it be conceived that something could veil Him when He is nearer to you than anything else?

How can it be conceived that something could veil Him when were it not for Him, nothing would have existed?

What a marvel! How could being appear in nonbeing? And how could an originated thing be established alongside the One who has the attribute of ancientness? (*Al-Ḥikam al-ʿaṭāʾiyya*, 16).

Allah cannot be conceived by the senses yet He is more manifest than anything. Nothing can hide Him from reason and insight. He manifests everything that comes into being and is manifest through His effects in every existing thing, "Indeed, in the alternation of the night and the day and in what Allah has created in the heavens and the earth are signs for a people who fear Allah" (Yūnus 10:6). He cannot be veiled by anything because there is nothing with Him, He is the nearest to everything, and He is the Creator of everything. Nothing that is of possible existence may exist without the action of the Creator, who is of necessary existence. Every creature is originated and ephemeral whereas the Creator is ancient and everlasting.

How different is one who seeks proof from Him and one who seeks proof of Him! One who seeks proof from Him has learned the truth from its owner and has established the matter from its source. Seeking proof of Him stems from not arriving to Him. Otherwise, when was He ever absent for proof of Him to be sought? Or

> when was He ever distant for effects to guide to Him? (*Al-Ḥikam al-ʿaṭāʾiyya*, 29).

The person who is close to Allah has Him as his source of knowledge and guidance on anything. One who seeks anything other than Allah for proof of Allah is remote from Him. Allah is never absent for proof of Him to be needed and is never distant for His effects in the creation to be needed to draw close to Him.

> The Real One is not veiled; rather, it is you who are veiled from seeing Him. For if anything were to veil Him, that veil would cover Him. If there were a cover of Him, it would be a limitation to His being. Any limitation to a thing is a subduer of it, "And He is the subduer over His servants" (al-Anʿām 6:18) (*Al-Ḥikam al-ʿaṭāʾiyya*, 33).

Nothing could veil Allah because the veiler has authority over the veiled yet no one has authority over Allah who has absolute power over everything. It is the servant's shortcomings that veil him from seeing his Lord.

> Allah was and there was nothing with Him. He is now as He was (*Al-Ḥikam al-ʿaṭāʾiyya*, 37).

Allah was alone before the creation and He remains alone because the aloneness of the ancient Creator does not change by His creation of originated things.

> He has illuminated the outwards with the lights of His effects and He has illuminated the innermost beings with the lights of His attributes. For this reason, the lights of the outwards set whereas the lights of the hearts and innermost beings do not set. This is why it has been said:
>
> The daytime sun sets at night,

> But the sun of hearts never sets[1] (*Al-Ḥikam al-ʿaṭāʾiyya*, 104).

Allah has made the world visible by the sources of light that He created, such as the sun, but He has made the hearts of His servants see Him with the light of His attributes that He revealed to them. While created lights go down, the lights of knowing Him in the heart never set.

> Cling to the attributes of His Lordship and realise the attributes of your servanthood (*Al-Ḥikam al-ʿaṭāʾiyya*, 125).

Ascribe the attributes of Lordship to Him only and adorn yourself with the attributes of servanthood to Him.

> He has prohibited you from claiming what is not yours which belongs to other creatures. So how could He permit you to claim His attributes when He is the Lord of the worlds? (*Al-Ḥikam al-ʿaṭāʾiyya*, 126).

Allah has prohibited the servant from claiming other creatures' possessions, so He could not permit him to claim His attributes, being the Lord of all creation.

> It is not the existence of any being with Allah that veils you from Him, for there is nothing with Him. Rather, what veils you from Him is the illusion that there is something with Him (*Al-Ḥikam al-ʿaṭāʾiyya*, 137).

Noting could veil the servant from Allah because everything is made by Him, exists by His will, and is a sign pointing to Him. Forgetting this, such as when attributing the giving and taking to creatures and relying on means, is what keeps the servant remote

---

[1] The poetry is by al-Ḥallāj.

from His Creator.

> He has manifested everything because He is the Hidden and He has concealed the existence of everything because He is the Manifest (*Al-Ḥikam al-ʿaṭāʾiyya*, 139).

He is the Hidden, whom no senses nor faculty can perceive, and He manifested everything. So everything He created, even if hidden to much of His creation, is manifest relative to Him. As He manifested everything, every manifest thing is a sign pointing and guiding to Him. So, He is the Manifest, whose manifestation has no equivalent. This is the unique meaning of each of His two names, "the Manifest and the Hidden" (al-Ḥadīd 57:3).

> The Universes are permanent by Him making them so and they are annihilated by the oneness of His being (*Al-Ḥikam al-ʿaṭāʾiyya*, 141).

The worlds exist because Allah has brought them into existence and He preserves them. They are ephemeral, so neither preexistent nor eternal. He alone is ancient, preexistent, and eternal. He is also of necessary existence, so everything else is originated and of possible existence, having a beginning and an end, whereas "He is the First and the Last" (al-Ḥadīd 57:3).

> The Real One is veiled from you by His utmost nearness to you (*Al-Ḥikam al-ʿaṭāʾiyya*, 164).

Remoteness is usually the cause of veiling among the creation, but the Creator's veiling from His servants is due to His extreme nearness to them, not His remoteness from them. The extreme nearness of something to the eye makes it invisible. Allah said, "We created man and We know what his soul whispers to him, and We are nearer to him than his jugular vein" (Qāf 50:16).

> He is veiled from you due to the intensity of His

manifestation and He is hidden from sight due to the greatness of His light (*Al-Ḥikam al-ʿaṭāʾiyya*, 165).

Allah is totally manifest indirectly in His creation and signs yet He is totally hidden to direct vision because eyes cannot see His unique light, "Vision cannot attain Him but He attains all vision, and He is the Subtle, the Well-Acquainted" (al-Anʿām 6:103).

His effects indicate that He has names, His names confirm His attributes, and the confirmation of His attributes indicates the existence of His Being. It is impossible for an attribute to exist by itself (*Al-Ḥikam al-ʿaṭāʾiyya*, 250).

The creation confirms the Creator's beautiful names, which, in turn, express attributes and capabilities of Him. An attribute could not exist without what it describes, so those attributes necessitate the existence of the Divine Being. The creation is proof of the existence of the Creator.

He made you witness before He instructed you to testify. So, the outwards spoke of His divinity and the hearts and innermost beings realised His oneness (*Al-Ḥikam al-ʿaṭāʾiyya*, 257).

While the human being is still a sperm, Allah makes him testify to His Lording and his own servanthood, "And when your Lord took from the children of Adam—from their loins—their descendants and made them testify of themselves, 'Am I not your Lord?' They said, 'Yes, we have testified'" (al-Aʿrāf 7:172). This is the innate nature of tawḥīd with which the human being is created, "So set your face towards religion as an affirmer of Oneness; [this is] the innate nature (*fiṭra*) in which Allah has created man. There is no altering of Allah's creation" (al-Rūm 30:30). After Allah completes his creation and brings him forth into the world, He commands him to live in a way that confirms, in word and deed, his early testimony of Allah's Lordship and realises Allah's aim of creating him, which is for him to be a servant of Him, "I have not created the jinn and mankind except to worship Me" (al-Dhāriyāt 51:56). Everything in the world points the sound intellect to Allah's Lordship and that He is the One Creator.

> It is loathsome for a believer to seek his need from other than Allah (exalted is He) despite knowing His oneness and exclusive Lordship, as he hears Allah (exalted is He) saying, "Is Allah not enough for His servant?" (al-Zumar 39:36). This is loathsome coming from anyone, and it is even more loathsome coming from a believer. Let him remember the words of Allah (glorified is He), "O you who believe, fulfil the contracts" (al-Mā᾿da 5:1). Among the contracts that you have made with Him is that you do not submit your needs except to Him and do not rely on other than Him. This is necessitated by your acknowledgement of His Lordship on the Day of Measure, the Day of "Am I not your Lord?" (al-Aʿrāf 7:172). How can you recognise Him and affirm His oneness there but ignore Him here, when His bounty has repeatedly come to you and His favour and gifts have overwhelmed you? (*Al-Tanwīr*, 124).

The human being's testimony to Allah's Lordship before he is created is an acknowledgement that it is Allah who gives the servant what he needs. This testimony is confirmed by the succession of Allah's favours to the servant in this world. For a human being to seek his needs from or rely on anyone other than Allah is a loathed action because it is a breach of his pledge to Allah before he brought him into the world. It is even more loathsome when committed by a believer.

Whoever sees that Allah is his feeder, this realisation

> protects him from humiliating himself to creatures or having his heart inclining with love to anyone other than the Real King. Have you not heard the words of Ibrāhīm the intimate friend (peace be upon him), "It is He who gives me food and drink" (al-Shuʿarāʾ 26:79). He testified that Allah is alone in that and acknowledged His oneness in it (*Al-Tanwīr*, 150).

Allah is the true provider as the creatures are mere means in His hand through which He delivers His provision to each other.

> For the people of intimate knowledge, anything other than Allah may not be described as present or absent. For no one exits with Him as His oneness is confirmed, and no one other than Him can be absent because only that which is present may become absent (*Al-Tanwīr*, 163).

Allah alone is truly existent because only His existence is necessary and He exists by Himself without any means, whereas the existence of everything else is only possible and depends on Him to exist.

> Beware of the heart's obliviousness of Allah's (exalted is He) oneness. The first rank of those who remember Him is to be mindful of His oneness. Those who remember Him do not remember Him and are not granted unveilings except by that mindfulness. They are not expelled except due to their remembering Him while overcome by obliviousness (*Tāj al-ʿarūs*, 32).

No worship, including remembering Allah, is sound without being associated with continuous mindfulness of His oneness. Reflecting on His oneness makes the muwaḥḥid remember Allah and spiritual rewards descend on him. Heedlessness of His oneness annuls remembrance and keeps the rememberer remote from Allah.

ʿAlī Al-Khawwāṣ[1]

> When a servant's tawḥīd becomes perfect, he would not be able to claim authority over any creature because he sees everything to be Allah's (*Al-Ṭabaqāt al-kubrā*, vol. 2, 277).

The perfect muwaḥḥid is humble. He does not look down upon anyone because he sees himself and all creatures as equal servants of one Owner, Allah.

> When someone's tawḥīd becomes sound, he becomes free of hypocrisy, self-admiration, and anything that leads the person away from the way of guidance. This happens because he sees all actions and attributes not as his but as Allah's alone. No person should feel self-admiration for someone else's work or adorn himself with it (*Al-Ṭabaqāt al-kubrā*, vol. 2, 277-278).

The person whose tawḥīd is sound sees all of his good deeds and attributes as favours from Allah so he feels no self-admiration.

> Masterhood is not established except for Him and servanthood is not established except for you. The Master

---

[1] N/A-949 H / N/A-1542 CE. He was illiterate, so it was his student ʿAbd al-Wahhāb al-Shaʿrānī who documented his sayings, karāmas, and states. He is buried in Cairo. His name became suddenly known in the West in 2015 when Pope Francis quoted him in an encyclical (*Laudato si'*, 168-169.) The Pope quoted al-Khawwāṣ from a French book that inaccurately quotes the Arabic text. The Arabic source is ʿAbd al-Wahhāb al-Shaʿrānī's *Laṭāʾif al-minan wa al-akhlāq*, 606. The text is about *samāʿ* (listening to music) and how the Sufi state of ecstacy could result from hearing various sounds in the environment. Although the French source attributes the saying to al-Khawwāṣ, the context in al-Shaʿrānī's book makes me incline to think it is a commentary by al-Shaʿrānī on words by his Shaikh that he had just quoted.

cannot be owned and a servant cannot own (*Al-Ṭabaqāt al-kubrā*, vol. 2, 278).

Allah is the only master and everyone else is a servant. The Master owns and is never owned whereas a servant is owned and never owns.

ʿAbd al-Wahhāb al-Shaʿrānī[1]

I once heard a voice utter the following words, "When you prostrate to pray, say, 'Glory be to Him of whose greatness all that creatures have known is like an atom in the air that has no ceiling and no ground'" (*Al-Qawāʿid al-kashfiyya*, 46).

Everything that creatures can ever know about the greatness of the Creator is extremely small.

The person who understands the Almighty's words, "There is nothing like Him" (al-Shūrā 42:11), exalts the Real One (glorified and high is He) over the attributes of His creation and everything that occurs to the mind (*Al-Qawāʿid al-kashfiyya*, 47).

The verse indicates the necessity of not likening Allah to any of His creatures' attributes and any image that may occur to the mind.

[The people of unveiling and transmission agree that] whatever crosses your mind, Allah is different from it. The most that intellects can comprehend, even if broadly, are bodies, essences, and accidents. Yet it is known that Allah is not a body, essence, or accident. So a servant cannot truly know His Lord without remaining ignorant of His reality. The Almighty said, "They do not encompass Him in knowledge" (Ṭāhā 20:110) (*Al-Qawāʿid al-kashfiyya*, 46).

---

[1] 898-973 H / 1493-1565 CE. He was born in Qalqashanda in Qalyūbiyya, Egypt. His father died when he was younger than ten, so when he became twelve, he went to Cairo and lived in the Abū al-ʾAbbās al-Ghamrī Mosque. He practised Sufism at the hands of Shaikh ʿAlī Al-Khawwāṣ. He is the author of over seventy books.

The people of spiritual experiences, i.e., Sufis, and the people of transmitted sciences, i.e., scholars in general, agree that it is impossible to imagine Allah. Intellects are created to comprehend created things, which are bodies, essences, and accidents. None of these apply to Allah Almighty. No matter how much a servant knows his Lord, he remains ignorant of His reality because it is beyond the limits of his knowledge and understanding.

> We do not call Him (exalted is He) what He did not call Himself. He called Himself "the First and the Last" (al-Ḥadīd 57:3), not "the one before and the one after" (*Al-Anwār al-qudsiyya*, 20-21).

We cannot know about Allah other than how He described Himself. Having described Himself as "the First" does not mean that there is someone after Him, and being "the Last" does not indicate that there was someone before Him.

ʿAbd Allah Ibn ʿAlawī al-Ḥaddād[1]

We know, profess, believe, confess, hold with certainty, and testify that there is no God except Allah, alone, without an associate. He is a great God, a majestic king. There is no Lord other than Him and no one worthy of worship besides Him. He is ancient and preexistent, everlasting and eternal. His firstness has no beginning and His lastness has no end.

Allah's ancientness means that He has always existed, and His everlastingness means that His existence has no end. He is the First who did not come into existence at a particular point, and He is the Last whose existence will never end.

He is alone and self-sufficient, "He has not begotten and has not been begotten, and there is no equal to Him" (al-Ikhlāṣ 112:3-4). He has no like and no equivalent, "there is nothing like Him, and He is the hearing, the seeing" (al-Shūrā 42:11). He Almighty is exalted over time, space, and resembling the worlds. Directions do not encompass Him and He is not subject to events. He is established on the Throne as He described it and in the sense He intended, an establishment that is befitting of the majesty of His exaltation and elevation of His glory and pride.

We cannot understand His establishment on the Throne but we believe in whatever He meant by that and that it is befitting of

[1] 1044-1132 H / 1634-1720 CE. He was born in Tarim in Hadhramaut, Yemen, where he also died and was buried. He lost his sight while a small boy. One of his Shaikhs was al-Ḥabīb ʿUmar Ibn ʿAbd al-Raḥmān al-ʾAṭṭās. He authored several works.

Him.

He (exalted is He) is near to every existing thing. He is closer to the human being than his jugular vein. He is watchful over and a witness to everything. He is everliving and vigilant, "neither slumber nor sleep overtakes Him" (al-Baqara 2:255), "Originator of the heavens and the earth. When He decrees a matter, He only says to it, 'Be,' and it is" (al-Baqara 2:117), "Allah is the Creator of everything and He is guardian over everything" (al-Zumar 39:62). He (exalted is He) "has power over everything" (al-Baqara 2:20), "He knows of everything" (al-Baqara 2:29), "He encompasses everything in knowledge" (al-Ṭalāq 65:12), "He keeps count of everything" (al-Jinn 72:28), "and not an atom's weight in the earth or in the heaven escapes your Lord" (Yūnus 10:61), "He knows what enters the earth and what emerges from it and what comes down from the sky and what ascends into it; He is with you wherever you are; and Allah sees what you do" (al-Ḥadīd 57:4), "He knows the secret and what is more hidden" (Ṭāhā 20:7), "He knows what is on the land and in the sea; not a leaf falls but that He knows of it; and there is not a grain within the darknesses of the earth and no moist or dry thing but that it is written in a clear record" (al-Anʿām 6:59).

He (exalted is He) wills what beings exist and He manages events. No good or evil or benefit or harm exists except by His decree and will. What He wills happens and what He does not will does not happen. If all creatures joined forces to move or stop an atom in the universe without His will they would fail to do that (*Al-Naṣāʾiḥ al-dīnīyya*, 415–416).

Nothing happens or comes into existence other than by Allah's will.

Muḥammad Muḥammad Al-Kasnazān[1]

What is the meaning of the statement of tawḥīd, "whoever says 'there is no God except Allah' enters paradise"[2]? How does the person who says "there is no God except Allah" enter paradise"? The testimony "there is no God except Allah" is inclusive of everything: surrender, sacrifice, giving witness, praying, fasting, commanding what is good and prohibiting what is bad, spending in Allah's cause, prostrating to Allah (exalted is He) day and night, kneeling to Allah (exalted is He), and sacrificing the soul; sacrificing the soul is the last stage (*Sermon,* 30 October 2012).

The above ḥadīth of the Prophet (PBUH) does not mean that merely uttering the testimony of tawḥīd, "There is no god save Allah", admits the servant into paradise. It, rather, means combining the testimony of the tongue with belief in the heart and good deeds. So tawḥīd means fulfilling the devotional and transactional obligations of Islam.

---

[1] 1357-1441 H / 1938-2020 CE. He was born in the village of Karbchna in Sulaymāniyya, northern Iraq. After the death of his father, Shaikh ʾAbd al-Karīm, in 1978, he succeeded him to the Shaikhdom of Ṭarīqa ʾAliyya Qādiriyya Kasnazāniyya. In each of the first three years of his Shaikhdom, he entered a forty-day-long retreat. He had great love for performing dhikrs, praying, and worshipping in general. He continued to perform night worships even when he was over eighty years old. He is the Shaikh on whose hands I started to practise Sufism. He generously privileged me with his close companionship. I learned so much from him about Sufism as a moral and behavioural system, spiritual path, thought, and spiritual states. One of his publications is the remarkable *Mawsūʿat al-kasnazān fīmā aṣṭalaḥ ʿalayh ahl al-taṣṣawuf wa al-ʿirfān*, a unique twenty-four-volume encyclopaedia on Sufism.

[2] Abū Yaʿlā al-Mawṣillī, *Al-Musnad,* 3899.

> You first start with the testimony of tawḥīd. This testimony means that the human being becomes a witness of himself. When you say, "There is no God except Allah, Muḥammad is the Messenger of Allah", you must say it with your tongue, your heart, and all of your body, in complete faith and total belief. This is how you must say the testimony. You must then start applying what the Messenger (PBUH) conveyed: his sayings, actions, and states (*Sermon,* 12 August 2013).

Tawḥīd is a testimony by the tongue, faith in the heart, and application of all teachings of the Prophet (PBUH).

> Tawḥīd is the foundation of faith. The foundation of the creed is the testimony, "I testify that there is no God except Allah and I testify that our Master Muḥammad is the Messenger of Allah (PBUH)" (*Sermon,* 12 August 2013).

Affirming the oneness of Allah and accepting the prophethood of Muḥammad (PBUH) is the foundation of faith and the creed.

> Your religion, faith, and belief have a set of requirements that starts with the statement of tawḥīd and concludes with "and they spend out of what We have provided for them" (al-Baqara 2:3) (*Sermon,* 12 August 2013).

Religion is based on credal foundations, the first of which is tawḥīd, and behavioural foundations of good deeds, one of which is spending in Allah's cause. The importance of the latter is manifested in the occurrence of this verse, "and they spend out of what We have provided for them", six times in the Qur'an (al-Baqara 2:3, al-Anfāl 8:3, al-Ḥajj 22:35, al-Qaṣṣaṣ 28:54, al-Sajda 32:16, and al-Shūrā 42:38) and the existence of many other verses that urge the believer to spend in Allah's cause. One sign of the importance of spending in Allah's cause is that the Qur'an mentions it in the chapter of Baqara in eighteen successive verses, 261-267 and 270-280, separated by only two other verses.

> You must repeat the following dhikr after your prayers so that you may take a lesson from it, "Allah is present with me, Allah sees me, Allah is a witness on me. Allah is with me, Allah is my helper, and He is encompassing of all things" (*Sermon,* 22 January 2010).

Shaikh Muḥammad al-Muḥammad said that this dhikr is from ʿAbd al-Qādir al-Jīlānī, which he received from Shaikh Maʿrūf al-Karkhī. In the early 1990s, our Shaikh added it to the dhikrs of Ṭarīqa Kasnazāniyya to be recited three times after each of the five obligatory prayers. This dhikr helps the rememberer to maintain continuous consciousness that Allah is everpresent all the time and everywhere and that He is capable of everything.

I would like to conclude the quotes from my honourable Shaikh with a vision he saw about the testimony of tawḥīd. He saw a buried body that had completely turned into dust. A weak light started to flow through the blood vessels until it reached half of the body before retreating. He was told that this was the light of infancy, the light of innocence. Then ugly red fire spread throughout the entire body. He was told that this was the fire of Satan. Then an unparalleled white light whose brilliance is indescribable started to spread in the body's circulatory system from the head until it reached the feet, repelling the ugly red fire. He was told that this beautiful light was the light of "there is no god except Allah". When a person recites this dhikr, it extinguishes the fire of Satan and spreads in the body, protecting it from the Fire (*Sermon,* 12 May 2000).

This vision is an embodiment of the Messenger's (PBUH) description of the dhikr of "there is no god except Allah" as repelling the Fire from the one who recites it, "Allah has prohibited for the Fire he who says 'there is no god except Allah', seeking Allah's pleasure".[1]

[1] Al-Bukhārī, *Al-Ṣaḥīḥ,* 419.

Epilogue

I hope that I have succeeded in presenting a clear and sufficient picture of the concept of tawḥīd according to Sufis and how they excelled in describing it in detail in their speeches and writings.

As we have seen, Sufis do not have a different understanding of tawḥīd to that of other Muslim scholars. But as they train the self to acquire the finest manners with Allah, people, and creatures as a whole, rather than accepting the minimum requirements of religion, Sufis also seek the highest degree of tawḥīd and urge Muslims to follow suit. They speak, for instance, of the necessity that the servant maintains continuous consciousness that Allah is always with him, nothing happens without His permission, and He is the real cause of every happening, outward or inward. For Sufis, this incessant consciousness of Allah, His names, and His attributes is one state of tawḥīd.

The destination of the Sufi journey is spiritual annihilation in Allah. This is the highest degree of tawḥīd because it means achieving total servanthood and having absolute submission to the Lordship of Allah, the only God. As beautifully described by Shaikh ʿAbd al-Qādir al-Jīlānī (may Allah sanctify his secret), this spiritual journey starts with the tawḥīd by the tongue that "There is no God except Allah" and ends with the tawḥīd by witness that "There is no God except You".

This is *al-tawḥīd ʿinda al-ṣūfiyya* (tawḥīd according to Sufis).

Glossary

This is how technical Sufi and other Arabic terms are translated in this book.

ʿAjja wa Jalla: majestic and exalted is He
ʿAraḍ: accident (n.)
ʿĀrif: intimate knower
ʿIrfān: intimate knowledge
Abad: eternity
Abadī: eternal
Athar: effect/trace
Azalī: preexistent
Bāṭin: inward (n.); hidden (adj.)
Bāṭin (attribute of Allah): Hidden (adj.)
Dāʾim: everlasting
Ḍahir: outward (n.); manifest (adj.)
Ḍahir (attribute of Allah): Manifest (adj.)
Dhāt: being
Ḍidd: opposite
Fanāʾ: annihilation
Ḥadath: origination
Ikhlāṣ: sincerity
ʿIlm: knowledge
Ishāra: allusion
Ism (of Allah): name
Kayyafa: ascribed condition to
Maʿrifa: intimate knowledge
Mushāhada: witnessing
Muwaḥḥid: affirmer of Oneness
Nadd: peer
Qadīm: ancient
Qidam: ancientness
Sabab: means
Shabīh: like
Ṣifa (of Allah): attribute

Ṣamad: Self-sufficient
Ṣidq: truthfulness
Subhānah: glory be to Him
Ta'ālā: exalted is He
Ta'ṭīl: denying the ancientness of Allah's names and attributes
Taḥqīq: realisation
Tajrīd: abandonment of means, i.e., seeing nothing other than Allah in and behind everything
Tamthīl: likening Allah to anything
Tanzīh: exaltation
Taqwā: piety
Tasbīḥ: glorification
Tawakkul: trust; reliance
Tawḥīd (concept): Oneness; oneness of Allah
Tawḥīd (practice): affirmation of Oneness
Waḥidiyya: Oneness
Waḥdāniyya: Oneness
Wajd: ecstasy
Yaqīn: certitude
Zuhd: renunciation

References

ʿAbd al-Jabbār Ibn Aḥmad, Al-Qāḍī. *Sharḥ al-uṣūl al-khamsa*. Edited by ʿAbd al-Karīm ʿUthmān. Cairo: Maktabat Wahba, 1996.

ʿAbd al-Qāhir al-Baghdādī, Abū Manṣūr. *Al-Farq bayn al-firaq wa bayān al-firqa al-nājiya minhum*. Edited by Muḥammad Al-Khashat. Cairo: Makatabat Ibn Sīnā, 1988.

Abū Ṭālib al-Makkī, Muḥammad. *Qūt al-qulūb*. Edited by Maḥmūd Al-Riḍwānī. Cairo: Dār al-Turāth, 2001.

Abū Yaʿlā al-Mawṣillī, Aḥmad. *Al-Musnad*. Edited by Ḥusayn Asad. Damascus: Dār al-Maʾmūn Lil-Turāth, 1986.

Aḥmad Ibn Ḥanbal. *Musnad al-Imām Aḥmad Ibn Ḥanbal*. Edited by Shuʿayb al-Arnaʾūṭ et al. 50 vols. Beirut: Muʾassasat al-Risāla, 1995-2001.

Al-Aṣfahānī, Abū Nuʿaym. *Ḥilyat al-awliyāʾ wa ṭabaqāt al-aṣfiyāʾ*. Beirut: Dār al-Fikr Lil-Ṭibāʿa, 1996.

Al-Ashʿarī, Abu al-Ḥasan. *Maqālāt al-Islāmiyyīn wa ikhtilāf al-muṣallīn*. Edited by Muḥammad ʿAbd al-Ḥamid. Beirut: Al-Maktaba al-ʿAṣriyya, 1990.

Al-Bayhaqī, Aḥmad Ibn al-Ḥusayn. *Al-Madkhal ilā ʿilm al-sunan*. Edited by Muḥammad ʿAwwāma. Cairo: Dār al-Yusr, 2017.

———. *Kitāb al-zuhd al-kabīr*. 11 vols. Beirut: Muʾassasat al-Kutub al-Thaqāfiyya, 1987.

Al-Bukhārī, Muḥammad. *Al-Adab al-mufrad*. Edited by Muḥammad al-Albānī. Beirut: Dār al-Ṣiddīq, 2000.

———. *Al-Ṣaḥīḥ*. Edited by ʿAbd al-Qādir al-Ḥamad. 3 vols. Riyadh: ʿAbd al-Qādir al-Ḥamad, 2008.

Al-Daylamī, Abū Shujāʿ. *Al-Firdaws bi maʾthūr al-khiṭāb*. Beirut: Dār al-Kutub al-ʿIlmiyya, 1986.

Al-Dimashqī, Arslān. “Risāla fī al-tawḥīd.” In *Al-Shaikh Arslān al-Dimashqī*, edited by ʿAzza Ḥaṣriyya. Damascus: Ḥaṣriyya, ʿAzza, 1965.

Al-Ghazālī, Abū Ḥāmid. *Iḥyāʾ ʿulūm al-dīn*. Beirut: Dār Ibn Ḥazm, 2005.

———. *Mishkāt al-anwār wa miṣfāt al-asrār*. Edited by ʿAbd al-ʿAzīz Al-Sayrawān. Beirut: ʿĀlam al-Kutub, 1986.

Al-Ḥaddād, ʿAbd Allah Ibn ʿAlawī. *Al-Naṣāʾiḥ al-dīniyya wa al-waṣāyā al-ʾīmāniyya*. Beirut: Dār al-Ḥāwī, 1999.

Al-Ḥākim al-Nisābūrī, Muḥammad. *Al-Mustadrak ʿalā al-ṣaḥīḥayn*. Edited by Muṣṭafā ʿAṭā. Beirut: Dār al-Kubut al-ʿIlmiyya, 2002.

Al-Ḥallāj, Al-ḥusayn Ibn Manṣūr. *Dīwān al-Ḥallāj*. Edited by Bāsil ʿŪyūn Al-Sūd. Beirut: Dār al-Kubut al-ʿIlmiyya, 2013.

Al-Ḥamīda, Ḥamad. "Ru'yat Allah ta'ālā fī al-ākhira wa mawqif ahamm al-firaq al-Islāmiyya minhā." *Al-Majalla al-'Arabiyya li al-dirāsāt al-Islāmiyya wa al-shar'iyya* 7, no. 24 (2023): 43-58.

Al-Hujwīrī, 'Alī Abū al-Ḥasan. *Kashf al-maḥjūb*. Edited by Is'ād Qindīl. Cairo: Al-Majlis al-A'lā lil-Thaqāfa, 2007.

Al-Jāmī, 'Abd al-Raḥmān. *Nafaḥāt al-uns min ḥaḍarāt al-quds*. Cairo: Al-Azhar, 1989.

Al-Jīlānī, 'Abd al-Qādir. *Al-Fatḥ al-rabbānī wa al-fayḍ al-raḥmānī*. Cologne: Al-Jamal, 2007.

———. *Futūḥ al-ghayb*. Edited by 'Abd al-'Alīm Al-Darwīsh. Damascus: Dār al-Hādī, 2007.

———. *Purification of the Mind (Jilā' al-khāṭir) – Third Edition: Sermons on Drawing Near to God*. Translated by Shetha Al-Dargazelli and Louay Fatoohi. 3 ed. Birmingham, UK: Safis Publishing, 2021.

Al-Junayd al-Baghdādī, Abū al-Qāsim. *Rasā'il al-Junayd*. Edited by 'Alī 'Abd al-Qādir. Cairo: Bur'ī Wajdāy, 1988.

Al-Kalābādhī, Abū Bakr. *Al-Ta'arruf li-madhhab ahl al-taṣawwuf*. Cairo: Maktabat al-Khānjī, 1994.

Al-Kasnazān, Shaikh Muḥammad Al-Muḥammad. *Mawsū'at al-kasnazān fīmā asṭalaḥ 'alayh ahl al-taṣṣawuf wa al-'irfān*. Damascus: Dār al-Maḥabba, 2005.

Al-Nasā'ī, Aḥmad Ibn Shu'ayb. *Al-Mujtabā min al-sunan*. Edited by Farīq Bayt al-Afkār al-Dawliyya. Riyadh: Bayt al-Afkār al-Dawliyya, 1999.

Al-Niffarī, Muḥammad Ibn 'Abd al-Jabbār. *Al-Mawāqif*. Edited by Arthur Arberry. Cairo: Maktabat al-Mutannabī, 1935.

———. *Al-Mukhāṭabāt*. Edited by Arthur Arberry. Cairo: Maktabat al-Mutannabī, 1935.

Al-Qurṭubī, Muḥammad. *Al-Asnā fī sharḥ asmā' Allah al-ḥusnā*. 2 vols. Tanta: Dār al-Ṣaḥaba Lil-Turāth bi-Ṭanta, 1995.

Al-Qushayrī, Abū al-Qāsim. *Al-Risāla al-qushayriyya*. Edited by 'Abd al-Ḥalīm Maḥmūd and Maḥmūd Ibn al-Sharīf. Cairo: Maṭābi' Mu'assasat Dār al-Sha'b, 1989.

Al-Rāzī, Fakhr al-Dīn. *Al-Tafsīr al-kabīr*. 32 vols. Beirut: Dār al-Fikr lil-Ṭibā'a wa al-Nashr wa al-Tawzī', 1981.

Al-Rifā'ī, Aḥmad. *Ḥāl ahl al-ḥaqīqa ma'ā Allah*. Edited by Aḥmad Al-Mazīdī. Beirut: Dār al-Kubut al-'Ilmiyya, 2004.

———. *Ḥikam al-Rifā'ī*. Beirut: Al-Ma'ba'a al-Adabiyya, 1883.

Al-Sā'ī, 'Alī Ibn Anjab. *Akhbār al-Ḥallāj*. Edited by Muwaffaq Al-Jabr. Damascus: Dār al-Ṭalī'a, 1997.

Al-Sakandarī, Ibn ʿAṭāʾ Allah. *Al-Ḥikam al-ʿaṭāʾiyya.* Edited by ʿAbd al-Majīd al-Sharnūbī. Damascus: Dār Ibn Kathīr, 1989.

———. *Al-Tanwīr fī isqāṭ al-tadbīr.* Edited by Muḥammad Al-Shaghūl. Cairo: Al-Maktaba al-Athariyya lil-Turāth, 2007.

———. *Laṭāʾif al-minan.* Edited by ʿAbd al-Ḥalīm Maḥmūd. Cairo: Dār al-Maʿārif, 2006.

———. *Tāj al-ʿarūs wa uns al-nufūs.* Edited by Maktab al-Rawḍa al-Sharīfa lil-Baḥth al-ʿIlmī. Cairo: Al-Maktaba al-Athariyya lil-Turāth, 2006.

Al-Shaʿrānī, ʿAbd al-Wahhāb. *Al-Anwār al-qudsiyya fī maʿrifat qawāʿid al-ṣūfiyya.* Edited by Ṭāha ʿAbd al-Bāqī and Muḥammad Al-Shāfiʿī. Cairo: Maktabat al-Maʿārif, 1988.

———. *Al-Qawāʿid al-kashfiyya al-muwaḍḍiḥa li-maʿānī al-ṣifāt al-ilāhiyya.* Edited by Aḥmad Darwīsh. Damascus: Dār al-Taqwā, 2009.

———. *Al-Ṭabaqāt al-kubrā.* Edited by Aḥmad Al-Sāyiḥ and Tawfīq Wahba. Cairo: Maktabat al-Thaqāfa al-Dīniyya, 2005.

———. *Laṭāʾif al-minan wa al-akhlāq fī wujub al-taḥadduth bi niʿmat Allah ʿalā al-iṭlāq.* Edited by Aḥmad ʿĪnāya. Damascus: Dār al-Taqwā, 2004.

Al-Shībī, Kāmil Muṣṭafā. *Al-Ṣila bayn al-taṣawwuf wa al-tashayyuʿ.* Cairo: Dār al-Maʿārif, 1969.

Al-Sulamī, Abū ʿAbd al-Raḥmān Muḥammad. *Ṭabaqāt al-ṣūfiyya.* Edited by Muṣṭafā ʿAṭā. Beirut: Dār al-Kutub al-ʿIlmiyya, 1998.

Al-Tirmidhī, Muḥammad. *Al-Jāmiʿ al-kabīr.* Edited by Bashshār Maʿrūf. 6 vols. Beirut: Dār al-Gharb al-Islāmī, 1996.

Al-Ṭūsī, Abū Naṣr al-Sarrāj. *Al-Lumaʿ fī al-taṣawwuf.* Edited by ʿAbd al-Ḥalīm Maḥmūd and Ṭahā Surūr. Baghdad: Maktabat al-Muthannā, 1960.

ʿAlī Ibn Abī Ṭālib. *Nahj al-balāgha.* Edited by ʿAbd Allah Al-Ṭabbāʿ and ʿUmar Al-Ṭabbāʿ. Beirut: Muʾassasat al-Maʿārif, 1990.

Fatoohi, Louay. *Al-Taṣawwuf fil-ṭarīqa al-ʿalīyya al-qādiriyya al-kasnazāniyya: manjahjun taʿbīqī lil-jānib al-rūḥī lil-Islām.* Birmingham: Dār al-Ṭarīqa, 2020.

———. *A Life of love for the Prophet Muḥammad (PBUH): a biography of Shaikh Muḥammad al-Muḥammad al-Kasnazān.* Birmingham: Safis Publishing, 2022.

———. *The Prophet Joseph in the Qur'an, the Bible, and history: a new detailed commentary on the Qur'anic chapter of Joseph.* Kuala Lumpur: Islamic Book Trust, 2005.

———. *Shaikh Muhammad al-Muhammad al-Kasnazan al-Husayni: a life in the footsteps of the best of lives.* Birmingham: Safis Publishing, 2020.

Francis, Pope. *Laudato si' (Praise be to You): on care for our common home.* Encyclical Letter. Vatican: Vatican Press, 24 May 2015, 2015.

Ibn Abū ʿĀṣim, Aḥmad. *Al-Āḥād wa al-mathānī*. Riyadh: Dār al-Rāya, 1991.

Ibn al-Nadīm, Muḥammad Ibn Isḥāq. *Al-Fihrast*. Beirut: Dār al-Maʿrifa, undated.

Ibn al-Wardī, Zayn al-Dīn. *Tārīkh Ibn al-Wardī*. Al-Najaf: Al-Maṭbaʿa al-Ḥaydariyya, 1969.

Ibn ʿArabī, Muḥyī al-Dīn. *Al-Futūḥāt al-makkiya*. Edited by Aḥmad Shams al-Dīn. Beirut: Dār al-Kutub al-ʿIlmiyya, 1999.

———. *Al-Tajalliyāt al-ilāhiyya*. Edited by ʿUthmān Yaḥyā. Tehran: Markaz Nashr Dānshgāhī, 1988.

———. *Al-Waṣāyā*. Damascus: Dār al-Imān, 1988.

Ibn Māja, Muḥammad. *Al-Sunan*. 5 vols. Damascus: Dār al-Risāla al-ʿIlmiyya, 2009.

Ibn Taymiyya, Taqiyy al-Dīn Aḥmad. *Al-Istiqāma*. Edited by Muḥammad Sālim. Riyadh: Jāmiʿat al-Imām Muḥammad Ibn Sʿūd al-Islāmiyya, 1991.

———. *Majmūʿ fatāwa*. Medina: Mujammaʿ al-Malik Fahad Li-Ṭibāʿat al-Muṣḥaf al-Sharīf, 2004.

Mālik Ibn Anas. *Al-Muwaṭṭaʾ (narrated by Yaḥyā b. Yaḥyā al-Laythī)*. 6 vols. Abu Dhabi: Muʾassasat Zāyid Ibn Sulṭān Āl Nhayyān al-Khairiyya, 2004.

Muslim, Abū al-Ḥusayn. *Al-Ṣaḥīḥ*. Edited by Muḥammad ʿAbd al-Bāqī. 5 vols. Cairo: Dār al-Ḥadīth, 1991.

Ṣabrī, Ḥusayn. *Ruʾyat Allah fī al-Islam*. Abū Dhabi: Al-Ḍiyāʾ, 2011.

Zarrūq, Abū al-ʿAbbās Aḥmad. *Qawāʿid al-taṣawwuf wa shawāhid al-taʿarruf*. Edited by Nizār Ḥammādī. Sharjah: Al-Markaz al-ʿArabī lil-Kitāb, undated.

www.ingramcontent.com/pod-product-compliance
Lightning Source LLC
Chambersburg PA
CBHW060252050426
42448CB00009B/1623
* 9 7 8 1 9 0 6 3 4 2 5 8 6 *